PRAISE FOR *THE NAVY SEAL PLAYBOOK*

"There are leadership and self-improvement books written by academicians, and there are those written by warriors. The former write from research, the latter from experience. There is much one can learn from research, but the lessons learned via challenging experiences are imprinted forever. They are life-changing. I have known and worked with Don for decades and he is a man who has tested the limits in so many endeavors... and succeeded. Whether you are looking for a similar path or want to excel at any endeavor, Don will lead you through the process with a lot less pain."

—Enrique "Ric" Prado, retired Chief of Operations at CIA's Counterterrorist Center and bestselling author of *Black Ops*

"In *The Navy SEAL Playbook,* my friend Don Mann has done what few authors can: turn elite experience into something you can actually use on a Monday morning. This isn't theory or hype—it's a field manual for winning when things get hard, fast, and uncertain. If you lead people, build teams, or carry responsibility that keeps you awake at night, this book belongs on your desk. Read it once for inspiration, then keep it close for execution."

—Jeff Tiegs, LTC, retired U.S. Army Special Forces, Delta Force Operator and President of Skull Games Solutions

"Don Mann has lived and continues to live by the lessons he puts forth in *The Navy SEAL Playbook.* For anyone seeking success, be it in civilian or military life, he provides valuable lessons on how to accomplish it. Having known and worked with Don for many years, I can assure you he epitomizes the ideals set forth in this book."

—Jeff Emde, author and retired CIA Operations Officer

"There are moments in life when we encounter ideas so powerful that they shift the way we see ourselves and the world around us. *The Navy SEAL Playbook* is one of those rare works. Rooted in the uncompromising discipline and resilience of the U.S. Navy SEALs, it offers not just strategies, but a way of living—a framework for achieving excellence in every area of life, whether in career, relationships, or health."

—Naomi Ray Fucci, U.S. Army Major Veteran

"What can the average person learn from a SEAL? Everything, as it turns out. Don has managed to distill the essence of the SEAL ethos into principles that can help any of us navigate a difficult career change, commit to a fitness goal, or simply be a better partner and parent. For fifty years, I have seen Don Mann apply these values, whether it was under fire, during a tough period of transition, or simply planning a weekend camping trip. His integrity is his anchor, and his tenacity is a force of nature. He is not just writing about principles, he is writing about the way he lives."

—Dr. Walter C. Rustmann, Col, FS CDR
147 Medical Group, USAF, Retired

THE NAVY SEAL PLAYBOOK

PRINCIPLES, PRACTICES & STRATEGIES FOR ACHIEVING SUCCESS

DON MANN
US NAVY SEAL (Ret)

Hatherleigh Press, Ltd.

62545 State Highway 10, Hobart, NY 13788, USA

hatherleighpress.com

THE NAVY SEAL PLAYBOOK

Library of Congress Cataloging-in-
Publication Data is available.

ISBN: 978-1-961293-54-0

Cover and interior design by Carolyn Kasper

Printed in the United States

The authorized representative in the EU for product safety and compliance is Catarina Astrom, Blästorpsvägen 14, 276 35 Borrby, Sweden. info@hatherleighpress.com

10 9 8 7 6 5 4 3 2 1

CONTENTS

"The only easy day was yesterday."

—Navy SEAL Aphorism

Every day presents new challenges—growth comes from embracing them.

INTRODUCTION

THE UNITED STATES NAVY'S SEA, AIR, AND Land (Navy S.E.A.L.) Teams, better known as the Navy SEALs, are among the most elite special operations forces in the world. Navy SEALs are driven by a profound sense of duty to their country, their team, and the mission at hand. Their purpose is rooted in selflessness, knowing that their actions directly impact the safety and success of others. This deep commitment fuels their ability to overcome challenges and make sacrifices, as they understand they are part of something far larger than themselves.

In this book, we delve into the core principles that drive Navy SEALs to extraordinary success and how *you* can apply these principles to your own life:

Commitment and Accountability

Success begins with unwavering commitment, even in the face of challenges. Navy SEALs understand that following through on promises and continually pushing themselves is essential to achieving their goals.

Clear Goals and Consistent Progress

Setting clear goals and consistently tracking progress is vital for growth. Pushing past comfort zones, staying accountable, and making consistent effort are the keys to success in both high-pressure situations and everyday life.

Growth Through Discomfort

True growth occurs when you embrace discomfort and push beyond your limits. This mindset drives Navy SEALs and is essential for overcoming personal barriers.

Surround Yourself with Excellence

To unlock your full potential, surround yourself with people who challenge you to be your best. Seek partners and mentors who demand excellence from you, and avoid those who let you coast.

Ownership and Responsibility

Take full responsibility for your personal growth and success. Just like Navy SEALs, don't wait for external motivation—be proactive, set long-term goals, and stay focused on your development.

Identifying Your Mission

Clearly define what truly matters and prioritize actions that lead to success.

Eliminating Distractions

Remove anything that does not contribute to achieving your mission.

Operate with a Mission Success Mindset

Approach every challenge with focus, discipline, and determination.

Navy SEAL Strategies

Through the application of these principles, you will be equipped with tools to help resolve situations in proactive ways:

Set clear, measurable goals. Break your goals into daily, weekly, and long-term objectives, and track your progress regularly.

Call out excuses and hold yourself accountable. Real accountability means confronting your excuses head-on and pushing through them.

Push each other beyond your comfort zones. Growth happens when you step outside of your comfort zone. Challenge yourself and those around you to expand your limits.

Devote yourself to your work/career. Fully commit to your work. Keep improving your skills, honor your promises, and remain dedicated to your professional growth. This foundation is critical for success in any career.

Prioritize your personal growth. Understand that your personal growth is your responsibility. Focus on constant self-improvement, even when it's uncomfortable.

Navy SEALs recognize that their legacy extends beyond the battlefield—it also resonates within their communities and families. Their personal mission is about creating a lasting impact, one that others can learn from and benefit from long after they've served. This sense of purpose transcends their time in service, as they aim to inspire others and contribute to the greater good.

A Navy SEAL's legacy may be built on the values of leadership, integrity, and courage—teaching others the principles that have guided their success, and motivating the next generation to embrace service, selflessness, and dedication to a cause greater than themselves.

1

COMMITMENT & ACCOUNTABILITY

Driven by a personal commitment to excellence, Navy SEALs do not settle for mediocrity. This mindset not only ensures their own success but also motivates their team to uphold the same high standards. Each individual's pursuit of peak performance elevates the team as a whole.

"Accept the challenges so that you can feel the exhilaration of victory."

— General George S. Patton

MISSION OBJECTIVES

In this chapter, we dive into the core principles that define Navy SEAL excellence: commitment, accountability, discipline, adaptability, decisiveness, and ownership. These are not abstract concepts; they are the foundation of peak performance under pressure.

Navy SEALs operate in environments where hesitation, excuses, or lack of preparation can cost lives. Understanding how to commit fully, act decisively, adapt quickly, and own every outcome ensures success in the most demanding circumstances.

These lessons are equally transformative. Whether in business, sports, or daily life, the ability to stay disciplined, prioritize long-term goals over short-term comfort, and respond creatively to unexpected challenges builds resilience, reliability, and confidence. This chapter will show how adopting a Navy SEAL mindset allows you to push past obstacles, manage stress, and achieve higher performance, both individually and within a team.

Learning Objectives

- Why unwavering commitment is more powerful than fleeting motivation.
- How discipline and daily habits create momentum toward success.

- Techniques for stress management, decision-making under pressure, and delayed gratification.
- The importance of adaptability, flexibility, and solution-focused thinking.
- How ownership and after-action reviews accelerate personal growth and team performance.

Commitment

Commitment is not something that comes and goes—it's a decision to follow through, no matter how difficult or uncomfortable the journey becomes. **Navy SEALs commit to their mission, their team, and their training, regardless of external circumstances or their current mood.** It's this unwavering commitment that allows them to push forward when motivation falters.

What keeps Navy SEALs moving forward is their commitment to their team, their purpose, and their ultimate goal. This is where they cultivate the mental toughness to push through adversity, without relying on fleeting motivation. They understand that true strength lies in their ability to keep going, even when motivation fades.

Discipline is a Requirement

Discipline is non negotiable in Navy SEAL culture. **Navy SEALs know that consistency and hard work are what allow them to reach their highest potential.**

The Navy SEAL mindset is clear: find solutions, not excuses. They rely on daily habits and routines that eliminate excuses altogether. Whether it's cold, rainy, or they're exhausted, the mission always comes first. This commitment extends to every aspect of their preparation and execution—training, planning, and performance are mandatory, not optional.

The ability to adapt and improvise is key to Navy SEAL success. When they face unexpected challenges, they don't let setbacks derail them. Instead, they quickly assess the situation, adjust their approach, and continue moving forward.

Living with purpose and discipline creates momentum. Every Navy SEAL knows that waking up each day with a clear mission and the self-discipline to execute it unlocks a level of potential that most people never reach. Navy SEALs live with a sense of purpose that fuels their daily actions, propelling them toward success and pushing them to achieve greatness.

Stress Management

High-stress situations are a given, but Navy SEALs are trained to manage stress in ways that allow them to stay focused and make critical decisions. Techniques like controlled breathing, mental rehearsal, and positive self-talk keep their minds clear even in the most intense moments. They know they must prioritize what's most important to make the greatest impact on mission success.

By consistently putting in extra effort, focusing on solutions, and preparing for the unexpected, Navy SEALs ensure that they are always ready for whatever comes their way. **This mindset is not just about surviving; it's about thriving, no matter how chaotic the situation may become.**

Excuses Solve Nothing, Action Solves Everything

Navy SEALs embrace a mindset that focuses on solutions instead of obstacles, always asking, "How can I?" rather than saying, "I can't." For Navy SEALs, the phrase, "Find a way or make a way" is not just a motto; it's a way of life. They understand that their actions and decisions directly impact their success and the success of their team and mission. When something goes wrong, they don't waste time pointing fingers or making excuses. Instead, they take responsibility and ask themselves, "What could I have done differently?"

This approach is ingrained into every level of Navy SEAL training. A Navy SEAL leader mentors their team by reinforcing the importance of taking ownership, even in difficult circumstances. When a team member faces a challenge, a Navy SEAL leader doesn't offer excuses or blame external factors. They guide their team to reflect on their own actions, fostering a mindset of accountability and self-improvement. **This focus on solutions, rather than excuses, ensures that the team can move forward with clarity and purpose.**

Decisiveness Under Pressure

Navy SEALs emphasize decisiveness, understanding that hesitation can weaken confidence, delay action, and increase vulnerability—especially in high-pressure situations. Their training is designed to develop the ability to make swift, confident decisions, trust instincts, and take action without second-guessing.

Navy SEALs are trained to make firm, well-informed decisions under extreme pressure, recognizing that timely action is often more valuable than waiting for the perfect solution. By embracing failure as part of the learning process, they sharpen their decision-making skills and maintain composure in high-stakes environments.

Training for Quick Decisions

Navy SEALs are conditioned to make rapid decisions in high-stakes environments where time is limited. Their training reinforces the importance of swift action, as indecision can lead to missed opportunities or dangerous consequences.

Through extensive training, Navy SEALs even develop an instinctive "flow state," where their actions become second nature. **By trusting their conditioning and experience, they make split-second decisions without overanalyzing, allowing them to respond effectively in critical moments.** In high-stress situations, Navy SEALs react almost reflexively, seamlessly coordinating mind and body. This ability to act quickly and decisively ensures precision, speed, and effectiveness in mission execution.

Leading with Confidence

A Navy SEAL leader must quickly assess a situation, determine the best course of action, and communicate it clearly. The team relies on the leader's decisiveness for direction, and this confidence strengthens morale and reinforces trust in the mission.

Decisiveness, combined with clear communication, is essential to a Navy SEAL's ability to perform under pressure, ensuring mission success and maintaining team cohesion. Whether in combat or leadership roles, the capacity to make confident, informed decisions is a hallmark of Navy SEAL excellence.

Delaying Gratification

Navy SEALs believe in more training than what might be necessary to ensure they are never caught off guard. **They understand that preparation is key to overcoming any obstacle, especially in high-stakes environments.**

Their approach to training is centered around a commitment to delayed gratification for long-term success, anticipating every potential challenge and planning for it meticulously. They believe that preparation eliminates excuses, pushing them to continuously improve and refine their skills to stay ahead of any scenario.

Preparing for the Worst

One of the core principles in Navy SEAL training is preparing for the worst-case possibility. Navy SEALs are not just prepared for the mission at hand; they prepare for the worst-case scenarios, including unexpected changes in the environment, enemy actions, or equipment failures. This level of readiness ensures that when things inevitably go wrong, they have a "Plan B" in place, making excuses irrelevant. **Instead of focusing on obstacles, Navy SEALs focus on solutions and adapt quickly.**

Before any mission, Navy SEALs conduct thorough briefings where they discuss potential contingencies and develop backup strategies. This extensive preparation doesn't just cover the predictable—like terrain or weather—but also includes what could happen if the enemy alters their strategy or if a critical piece of equipment fails. They embrace the idea that plans often fall apart in the field, so they remain agile and ready to improvise.

O.O.D.A.

The Navy SEAL mindset of creative problem-solving stems from their unpredictable training. They are taught to "train to uncertainty," which means they never know exactly what to expect. This uncertainty sharpens their ability to think on their feet, making them more adaptable when faced with unforeseen challenges. **The OODA loop (Observe, Orient, Decide, Act), a decision-making framework, is key to their success.** In moments of unpredictability, they observe the situation, orient themselves quickly, decide on the best course of action, and act decisively—often before the enemy can react.

Their ability to improvise comes from constant scenario-based training where they are faced with dynamic, ever-changing conditions. When things go awry, they adapt by using whatever resources are at hand, finding creative solutions to problems that could derail the mission. This mindset fosters the ability to think outside the box, where conventional tactics aren't enough, and unconventional methods must be employed.

Adaptability

Adaptability is a key factor in the success of Navy SEALs. Their ability to remain flexible, pivot quickly, and adjust to changing circumstances is essential in both training and operations. **By embracing change and viewing setbacks as opportunities for growth, Navy SEALs maintain their edge as one of the most elite and effective forces in the world.** Flexibility becomes a powerful tool in overcoming obstacles, ensuring success even in the most dynamic and unpredictable environments.

If a mission faces an unexpected tactical shift, such as a surprise ambush, Navy SEALs respond quickly by using their training and adaptability to adjust their approach or reposition to turn the situation around. This ability to embrace change ensures they remain resilient, always ready to tackle new challenges and seize opportunities, ensuring success in both training and real-world operations.

Flexibility

Flexibility is not just an individual trait—it's a defining characteristic of Navy SEAL teams. They understand that when one team member faces a setback, the entire team must adjust to support that person. **This team-first mentality ensures that obstacles never derail the mission.** Instead, the team adapts together, making necessary changes and providing mutual support throughout the process.

For instance, if a Navy SEAL struggles with a specific skill, they don't quit. Instead, they push through the challenge, refining their approach and learning from their mistakes. This adaptability not only strengthens them as individuals but also enhances the team as a whole.

Focus Forward

When challenges arise, Navy SEALs don't dwell on the failure; they focus on finding a way forward. Their solution-oriented mindset drives them to quickly adapt plans and strategies, keeping their attention on the end goal. **This enables them to remain adaptable and inventive in solving problems without becoming bogged down by frustration.**

For example, if an operation doesn't go as planned, the team doesn't waste time dwelling on mistakes. Instead, they swiftly assess the situation, adjust their approach, and stay focused on achieving their objectives.

Flexibility is also a key component of mental resilience. Navy SEALs are trained to cope with extreme stress and adversity, adjusting to changing conditions without losing momentum. Whether it's shifting weather, new intelligence, or changing mission parameters, they know that rigidity leads to failure. Flexibility enables them to adapt and accomplish the mission, no matter the unexpected challenges that arise.

They understand that flexibility not only helps them overcome immediate obstacles but can also lead to better results in the long run, as they learn to work with the situation rather than against it.

After Action Reviews (AARs)

After each mission or training exercise, Navy SEALs conduct After-Action Reviews (AARs) to assess what went well, what didn't, and how they can improve. This process highlights the importance of learning from mistakes and viewing setbacks as opportunities for growth, not obstacles.

During these debriefs, Navy SEALs reflect on their actions and decisions, understanding that failure is an essential part of the learning process. Rather than dwelling on mistakes, they focus on how to adjust and improve for future operations. They ask themselves critical questions: "What worked? What could I have done differently?" By carefully analyzing each mission, they continuously refine their strategies and approaches.

Ownership is a key aspect of the review process. Every team member, regardless of rank, is expected to reflect on their role and contribute to the assessment. **If something goes wrong—be it a communication breakdown, a tactical error, or an unforeseen challenge—the team collectively evaluates what could have been done better, ensuring no one shifts blame onto external factors.** This mentality promotes accountability and encourages ongoing improvement across the entire team.

A fundamental part of this process is brutally honest self-assessment. Navy SEALs strip away ego and critically examine their performance. They ask themselves tough questions: What went well? What could have been improved? What lessons did I learn? This kind of introspection is vital not only in combat but also in leadership, relationships, and personal growth.

Respect Your Failures

Failure is not a setback, but as an opportunity for valuable feedback. Each mission, whether successful or not, provides insights into what worked and what didn't. If something goes wrong, Navy SEALs don't blame external circumstances—they look inward and ask themselves how they can adapt and adjust to improve for next time.

A failure during a mission can feel disappointing, but Navy SEALs understand that it's part of the process. The debrief provides a space to analyze the situation, understand what went wrong, and identify steps to prevent it from happening again. This process strengthens mental resilience and allows the team to refine their skills for future challenges.

AFTER ACTION REVIEW

Mission Summary

Navy SEALs succeed because they combine personal commitment, mental toughness, disciplined habits, and accountability. They embrace challenges, take ownership of their actions, and remain flexible in the face of uncertainty. Every failure is an opportunity to learn, and every success is built on preparation, focus, and unwavering commitment.

Key Lessons for Reflection

Commitment: Follow through, even when motivation fades. Your team and your goals depend on it.

Discipline: Daily routines and consistent effort eliminate excuses and create reliability.

Decisiveness: Make informed decisions quickly, trust your instincts, and take action.

Adaptability and Flexibility: View setbacks as opportunities; adjust strategies without losing momentum.

Ownership and Accountability: Reflect honestly on failures, learn from them, and avoid blaming external factors.

Stress Management and Preparation: Anticipate challenges, prepare thoroughly, and focus on solutions rather than problems.

Confirmation of Learning:

- ✓ You understand that actions solve problems, not excuses.
- ✓ You can identify areas where commitment, discipline, and accountability can elevate your performance.
- ✓ You recognize the value of debriefing failures and successes to improve continuously.
- ✓ By internalizing these principles, you not only enhance your personal performance but also inspire those around you to embrace excellence. Like a Navy SEAL team, success is built on preparation, purpose, and unwavering commitment to the mission.

2

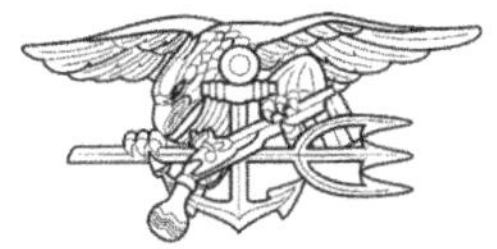

CLEAR GOALS & CONSISTENT PROGRESS

Setting clear goals and consistently tracking progress is vital for growth. Pushing past comfort zones, staying accountable, and making consistent effort are the keys to success in both high-pressure situations and everyday life.

"The greatest glory in living lies not in never falling, but in rising every time we fall."
—Ralph Waldo Emerson

MISSION OBJECTIVES

In this chapter, we focus on the Navy SEAL principles of setting clear goals, maintaining consistent progress, and embracing disciplined growth. We will explore how defining measurable objectives, pushing beyond comfort zones, and tracking progress builds not only individual capability but also strengthens team performance.

Navy SEALs operate in environments where small mistakes can have major consequences. Clear goals and consistent effort ensure they are always mission-ready, able to adapt to challenges, and capable of performing at their highest level under pressure.

For everyday life, these lessons are equally valuable. By setting SMART goals, prioritizing consistent effort over perfection, and learning from setbacks, you can achieve higher performance in work, fitness, personal development, and relationships. Whether you're leading a team, pursuing a personal milestone, or managing day-to-day challenges, the Navy SEAL approach to growth provides a blueprint for measurable, sustainable success.

Learning Objectives

- The Navy SEAL approach to continuous personal and team growth.
- The importance of consistency, endurance, and adaptability over perfection.
- Setting SMART goals and breaking them into actionable micro-steps.

- Using mental tools like mantras to maintain focus and drive.
- Turning setbacks into opportunities through reflection and learning.
- Cultivating self-discipline, resilience, and accountability to ensure steady progress.

The Navy SEAL Approach to Growth

Navy SEALs are committed to both personal development and team success, maintaining a strict regimen of physical fitness, tactical training, and mental conditioning. Every day presents an opportunity to refine their skills, strengthen their bodies, and sharpen their minds. This unwavering dedication ensures they are always ready for any challenge while upholding the core values that define their service.

Every experience—whether a triumph or a setback—is an opportunity for growth. Mistakes are not failures but valuable lessons that drive future success. They focus on extracting key insights, making strategic adjustments, and emerging stronger.

Consistency Requires Adaptability and Endurance

In Navy SEAL operations, the ability to sustain effort over long periods is more critical than perfect execution. Missions can last for hours or even days, requiring sustained performance through exhaustion and setbacks. Their success is built on endurance—on the ability to keep going despite challenges, not on getting everything right every time.

Yet missions rarely go as planned. Equipment malfunctions, environmental changes, and unforeseen challenges demand adaptability. Navy SEALs understand that flexibility and consistent performance matter more than executing a perfect strategy. Adjusting and responding effectively is always the priority.

A Navy SEAL doesn't expect to be flawless in every training session. What matters is showing up, giving full effort, and learning from every experience. Over time, this relentless commitment to consistency leads to mastery and success.

For Navy SEALs, overcoming obstacles is not about perfection but about resilience, adaptability, and unwavering effort. By focusing on progress, teamwork, and consistent execution, they continue to evolve, improve, and succeed—both as individuals and as a team.

Setting SMART Goals

Navy SEALs follow a structured approach to goal-setting, often using the **SMART criteria** to ensure that objectives are:

- **Specific:** Clearly defined with no room for ambiguity.

- **Measurable:** Progress is tracked to maintain accountability.
- **Achievable:** Goals are realistic yet challenging.
- **Relevant:** Directly contribute to personal growth or mission success.
- **Time-bound:** A set deadline ensures focused effort and measurable results.

For example, a Navy SEAL might set a goal to improve their 2-mile run time by 30 seconds within two months.

- **Specific** (improving run time)
- **Measurable** (30-second improvement)
- **Achievable** (based on current performance)
- **Relevant** (enhances operational fitness)
- **Time-bound** (achievable within two months)

Challenge Yourself

Navy SEALs never settle for the bare minimum—they push themselves beyond required standards to ensure peak performance when it matters most.

- **Train harder than the mission demands** to exceed expectations under pressure.
- **Stay sharp during downtime** rather than indulging in excessive relaxation—discipline and delayed gratification build resilience.

- **Think beyond immediate goals,** always striving for the next level of excellence.

Navy SEALs also structure their goals into macro and micro goals.

- **Macro Goals:** These long-term objectives provide direction and purpose, such as becoming a team leader, passing an elite qualification, or mastering a combat skill.
- **Micro Goals:** These smaller, actionable steps ensure steady progress, such as improving fitness scores, completing advanced training, or mentoring teammates.

By setting **challenging yet achievable** goals, Navy SEALs maintain motivation, direction, and a clear sense of purpose.

Setbacks Are Temporary

Setbacks are inevitable, but Navy SEALs remain committed to their goals by focusing on the value of hard work and prioritizing objectives.

- **Track progress** through training logs, performance metrics, or mentor feedback.
- **Adapt goals as needed** based on mission priorities, physical injury, or unexpected challenges while maintaining focus on the long-term vision.

- **Hold themselves accountable** through swim buddies, training partners, mentors, or team leaders who ensure they stay on track.

For example, if a Navy SEAL working on a fitness goal gets injured, they adjust their timeline and modify training to prioritize recovery while staying committed to their overall objective.

Consistency Over Perfection

Navy SEALs excel by focusing on what they can control and letting go of what they can't. Their mindset is built on focus, adaptability, and acceptance. Through mental conditioning, emotional control, and relentless training, they learn to direct their energy where it matters most. By embracing uncertainty, letting go of perfection, and concentrating on actionable steps, Navy SEALs remain calm, effective, and mission-ready in the most demanding environments.

Navy SEALs prioritize progress over perfection. They understand that continuous improvement is far more valuable than chasing an unattainable ideal. Every mission, workout, or challenge is an opportunity to refine their skills—regardless of whether the execution was flawless. This mindset keeps them motivated and prevents perfectionism from becoming a barrier to success.

Perfectionism can lead to hesitation and overthinking—two liabilities in high-pressure situations. Navy

SEALs are trained to make quick, decisive choices under stress. The pursuit of perfection can cause delays, second-guessing, or inaction. Instead, they focus on consistency, trusting their training and instincts to make the best possible decisions, even without complete information.

In combat, waiting for the perfect moment or an ideal plan can waste critical time. Navy SEALs are trained to act with confidence, focusing on effective, repeatable actions that drive the mission forward, even if the circumstances are less than perfect. **Progress is always more valuable than hesitation.**

Create Non-Negotiable Standards For Yourself

Navy SEALs create non-negotiable standards for themselves by setting clear expectations and holding themselves accountable to the highest level of performance. This approach ensures they never accept mediocrity and are always prepared to operate at their best, regardless of the situation. Their standards are unwavering, and they understand that to perform at the highest level, they must constantly challenge themselves.

For Navy SEALs, excellence is not just a goal—it's a mindset. It means constantly striving to be the best version of themselves in every aspect of their work and life. Whether it's a high stakes combat mission or routine training, Navy SEALs approach everything with the same level of commitment and dedication. They take immense pride in doing things at the highest level, and this pride drives them to continually push the boundaries of their abilities.

This relentless pursuit of excellence is built into Navy SEAL culture through a daily focus on improvement. Navy SEALs pay attention to even the smallest details, recognizing that mastery is a journey, not a destination. Whether in physical fitness, tactical training, or leadership skills, they consistently seek ways to refine their abilities and elevate their performance.

A Navy SEAL will always continue to perfect their shooting technique because he understands that true excellence is about the continuous pursuit of perfection, always striving for the next level of mastery. This commitment to self-improvement and mastery shapes their mindset, ensuring they are always ready to perform at the highest standard, no matter the challenge ahead.

Cultivate Self-Discipline

Mental toughness is at the core of the Navy SEAL mindset, and it all starts with mastering the art of self-discipline. Navy SEALs are trained to build this discipline by setting clear priorities and structuring their habits in a way that ensures they stay focused and composed, even in the most uncomfortable or high-pressure situations.

Self-discipline is not just about willpower; it's about making consistent decisions that align with their values and goals. **Navy SEALs understand that to succeed, they must prioritize what truly matters—whether it's the mission at hand, physical fitness, or mental readiness.** By honing this ability to stay focused on what's important, they eliminate distractions and unnecessary obstacles.

Through clear priorities and structured habits, Navy SEALs create a framework for success. They wake up with a clear plan and stick to it, even when fatigue or adversity sets in. This laser focus allows them to achieve peak performance in every area of life, whether in combat or everyday challenges.

It's not about being perfect; it's about being consistent, building mental toughness, and pushing forward despite the discomfort. The power of self-discipline is the key that unlocks your potential.

Mantras

Mantras are tools for redirecting focus, reinforcing mindset, and maintaining control under pressure. **In high-stress moments, complex thoughts are ineffective—mantras must be short, actionable, and easy to remember to provide immediate clarity and direction.**

Navy SEALs understand that endurance is more mental than physical. Their mental toughness is sometimes reinforced through the use of mantras, repeated aloud or internally, to remind themselves of their strength, resilience, and determination. These mantras help them push through adversity, even when physical and mental challenges seem insurmountable. A common mantra among Navy SEALs is, *"Every day is a chance to get stronger."* This phrase reflects their belief that growth comes from consistent effort and overcoming daily obstacles.

When fatigue sets in, repeating empowering phrases helps them override mental resistance and keep moving forward.

For example:

- **"I've done harder things before."** This reminds them of past challenges they've conquered, reinforcing confidence.
- **"This is temporary—keep moving."** A simple cue to focus on the next step rather than the pain.
- **"Stay focused. Move forward."** Keeps attention on the immediate task, blocking out distractions.
- **"I am strong. I am in control."** Reinforces inner strength and composure under pressure.
- **"Welcome the pain."** Encourages embracing discomfort as part of the process.
- **"Pain is temporary. Victory is forever."** Shifts focus from short-term struggle to long-term success.
- **"One step at a time."** Prevents overwhelm by breaking challenges into manageable actions.

- **"I've done it before. I can do it again."**
  Draws strength from past victories, reinforcing belief in their ability to overcome any challenge.

Courageous Actions

Mantras are more than words—they are a bridge between training and execution.

Beyond mantras, Navy SEALs embrace the concept of courageous action, recognizing that courage isn't the absence of fear but the ability to act despite it. **They see fear not as a barrier but as an opportunity—to grow, conquer doubts, and push beyond perceived limits.** By gradually exposing themselves to fear in controlled settings, they build resilience and confidence, preparing them to face high-stakes situations without hesitation.

Continuous Improvement and Growth

After each mission, Navy SEALs reflect on individual and team performance in debriefings, identifying areas of strength and opportunities for improvement. This constant feedback loop helps them stay agile, adaptable, and ready for future operations.

Debriefs also foster strong team cohesion. When a team faces a setback, they analyze the situation together, ensuring everyone is aligned on the lessons learned. This shared experience strengthens their bond and helps them work together more effectively. **By continuously learning from both successes and failures, Navy SEALs ensure that they never stop improving.**

The debrief process also allows leaders to reflect on their decision-making under pressure. If a leader made a decision that contributed to a failure, they use the debrief to learn from that experience and refine their decision-making skills for future high-stress situations.

Resilience Through Repetition

True resilience is forged through repetition. Navy SEALs understand that pushing beyond limits comes from exposure to difficult situations. Every grueling training evolution strengthens their ability to endure discomfort, fatigue, and setbacks. Over time, this rewires their brains for adaptability and toughness, making them more capable under extreme stress.

Navy SEAL training emphasizes endurance through physical training evolutions such as running with heavy loads, swimming in freezing water, and enduring long hours of physical exertion. **Their goal isn't flawless execution but sustained performance under extreme conditions.** By continuously pushing through discomfort, they prepare for the long haul, not just the short-term win.

Rely on Your Teammates

While individual excellence matters, Navy SEALs know that teamwork is the foundation of mission success.

A flawless performance by one person means little if the team as a whole falters. Supporting each other through mistakes, setbacks, and fatigue is more critical than personal perfection.

Navy SEALs rely on their teammates to maintain performance. When one member struggles, others step up. This mutual support system reinforces consistency, ensuring that no individual failure jeopardizes the overall mission.

Remember, Navy SEALs believe that small, consistent efforts lead to exponential improvement over time. Rather than aiming for a single moment of perfection, they focus on daily habits that build lasting strength, resilience, and skill. Even setbacks contribute to growth when they are met with persistence.

Identify Successes and Failures

Navy SEALs measure success not just by reaching goals but by learning from every challenge.

- **Celebrate achievements,** whether through personal reflection or team acknowledgment.
- **Debrief failures** to identify areas for improvement and refine future strategies.

When faced with doubt, Navy SEALs draw strength from past victories. By recalling times when they overcame adversity, they bolster their belief in their abilities. This mental reinforcement strengthens their resolve to succeed again, no matter the challenge at hand.

At the same time, Navy SEALs understand that not every decision will be perfect, but they know that indecision is far worse. They embrace mistakes not looking at them as failures, but as opportunities to learn and adjust, continuously improving by acting, learning, and refining their approach.

For Navy SEALs, goal-setting is more than a task—it's a disciplined, structured approach to continuous improvement. By defining clear objectives, breaking them into actionable steps, aligning them with team goals, and relentlessly tracking progress, they ensure that growth is constant. This commitment to excellence ensures they remain physically, mentally, and strategically prepared for any challenge, both in service and beyond.

AFTER ACTION REVIEW

Mission Summary

For Navy SEALs, growth and success are built on clarity, consistency, and deliberate effort. They understand that setbacks are temporary, consistency over time creates mastery, and disciplined reflection transforms mistakes into lessons for future success. Navy SEALs achieve excellence not by seeking perfection, but by relentlessly applying small, measurable actions toward clear goals.

Key Lessons for Reflection

Clarity of Goals: Define specific, measurable, achievable, relevant, and time-bound objectives.

Consistency Over Perfection: Focus on steady progress and sustained effort, even through discomfort and fatigue.

Adaptability and Endurance: Adjust strategies as circumstances change; persistence matters more than flawless execution.

Self-Discipline and Mental Tools: Use structured habits, priorities, and mantras to maintain focus under pressure.

Learning from Setbacks: Treat challenges as opportunities to reflect, adjust, and improve.

Team Integration: Individual effort contributes to collective success; support and accountability strengthen results.

Continuous Improvement: Break macro-goals into micro-goals, track progress, and refine actions based on feedback.

Confirmation of Learning

- ✓ You understand how structured goal-setting and disciplined effort drive long-term growth.
- ✓ You can identify the difference between chasing perfection and pursuing consistent improvement.
- ✓ You recognize the value of reflection, accountability, and adaptation in turning setbacks into progress.
- ✓ By internalizing these principles, you create a framework for continuous personal and team growth, ensuring you remain resilient, focused, and mission-ready—no matter the challenge.

3

GROWTH THROUGH DISCOMFORT

True growth occurs when you embrace discomfort and push beyond your limits. This mindset drives Navy SEALs and is essential for overcoming personal barriers.

"Success is not final, failure is not fatal: it is the courage to continue that counts."

—Winston S. Churchill

MISSION OBJECTIVES

This chapter explores the principle that true growth occurs outside your comfort zone. Navy SEALs know that pushing beyond perceived limits—physically, mentally, and emotionally—is the only way to develop resilience, adaptability, and unshakable mental toughness. For many readers, these principles are directly applicable to life outside of combat. Embracing discomfort in everyday challenges—whether in work, fitness, relationships, or personal growth—builds mental resilience, strengthens discipline, and enhances the ability to perform under pressure. By leaning into adversity instead of avoiding it, anyone can expand their limits, improve consistency, and achieve higher levels of success.

Learning Objectives

- How to push past limits through rigorous training and exposure to adversity.
- How to use discomfort as a tool for personal and team development.
- To build mental toughness and resilience to remain effective under extreme stress.
- To maintain performance under pressure through discipline, patience, and strategic recovery.
- How to turn obstacles into opportunities by reframing challenges as growth experiences.

Push Past Limits

Navy SEALs believe that true growth happens beyond the comfort zone. By continually pushing themselves through physical and mental hardship, they develop the capacity to endure whatever life throws their way—whether in training, on a mission, or in everyday struggles. This mindset fosters the resilience, adaptability, and toughness needed to thrive in the most demanding conditions.

Above all, Navy SEALs understand that commitment outweighs motivation. **Motivation is fleeting and unreliable, but commitment is an unwavering force—a constant drive that propels them forward, even in the toughest moments.**

Through continuous exposure to adversity, Navy SEALs learn that their bodies can endure much more than their minds initially believe. As they push their physical and mental limits in training, they build the mental toughness to keep going, even when faced with extreme pressure.

Welcome the Pain

"What doesn't kill us only makes us stronger." "The more sweat and tears you put into training, the less bloodshed in wartime." These military adages underscore a fundamental truth: rigorous preparation in times of peace minimizes casualties in real-world conflict.

During Hell Week, the temptation to quit offers fleeting relief, but those who persevere earn the opportunity to become Navy SEALs.

When discomfort reaches its peak, Navy SEALs rely on their teammates to push through. This camaraderie is at the core of the "get comfortable being uncomfortable" mindset. They understand they are never alone, and the unbreakable bond within the team strengthens their determination to keep going.

Pain is temporary, but mission success is paramount. Navy SEALs remain focused on their objective, no matter the hardship endured along the way.

Turning Obstacles Into Opportunities

Navy SEALs see obstacles as opportunities to grow stronger, more resilient, and more capable. This mental reframing—the ability to shift perspective and embrace adversity—allows them to thrive in the most demanding environments. **Instead of resisting hardship, they train their minds to welcome the grind and find strength in discomfort.**

For a Navy SEAL, cold water isn't just cold—it's a tool to build toughness. A long run isn't a burden; it's an opportunity to develop endurance. Every difficulty presents a lesson, and every challenge is a steppingstone toward greater mental and physical fortitude.

Navy SEALs set unbreakable personal standards and never lower the bar, no matter the circumstances.. Their ethos demands that they exceed minimum performance standards, constantly pushing the limits of their capabilities.

- **Set clear, non-negotiable** daily habits for self-improvement.
- **Never accept mediocrity**—meet or exceed your standards every time.
- **Hold yourself accountable**—no excuses, only action.

Push Through Discomfort—That's Where Growth Happens

Instead of seeing discomfort as something to avoid or fear, Navy SEALs are trained to view it as a challenge to overcome. "Get comfortable being uncomfortable." Navy SEALs know that discomfort is inevitable in high-stress situations—whether physical, mental, or emotional—and pushing through it is key to survival and effectiveness. Pain, exhaustion, and fear are natural reactions, but the more you can embrace discomfort, the less it can control you.

Navy SEALs stay focused on the end goal whether it's survival, mission completion, or success. This helps them maintain motivation and purpose in the most challenging times.

Mental Toughness and Resilience

Training emphasizes developing mental strength to push through pain, exhaustion, and discomfort. **Navy SEALs focus on the present moment rather than letting discomfort dominate their thoughts.** This mindset helps them stay calm and keep moving forward under pressure.

Whether it's physical or mental, Navy SEALs learn to embrace discomfort as part of the process of growth. They reframe pain as an opportunity to build resilience and focus on solutions, not complaints. When things get tough, they don't look for relief—they look for ways to succeed, no matter how uncomfortable it gets.

Training the mind to handle stress and uncertainty is key. Navy SEALs understand that adversity builds strength and prepares them for any situation. Their physical training is deliberately grueling, not just to test their bodies, but to build the mental toughness needed to endure hardship.

During brutal training exercises—whether it's long swims, obstacle courses, or carrying heavy gear—the goal isn't just physical fitness; it's about developing the ability to endure discomfort, fatigue, and pain without giving up.

Building Up Resistance to Adversity

Navy SEAL training is deliberately designed to expose the trainees to extreme stress, physical exhaustion, and mental strain. This process "inoculates" them against adversity, preparing them for even greater challenges ahead. Overcoming these trials builds confidence and desensitizes them to the fear and anxiety that discomfort often brings—allowing them to perform under pressure when it matters most.

A fundamental principle of Navy SEAL training is the refusal to quit. Whether enduring a brutal workout, a grueling mission, or a formidable life challenge, quitting is never an option. This mindset drives Navy SEALs to finish what they start—regardless of how painful or difficult the journey may be.

They understand that the key to overcoming discomfort lies within the mind. By training themselves to control their thoughts and emotions, they prevent discomfort from dictating their actions. Instead of viewing pain as a setback, they transform it into fuel for growth and performance.

Discomfort as a Tool

Navy SEALs don't seek discomfort for its own sake, but they recognize its value as a tool for personal and professional development. Whether in combat, high-pressure environments, or everyday challenges, learning to operate effectively under duress builds resilience and fortitude.

When exhaustion and pain set in, Navy SEALs reframe discomfort as a sign of progress. Each hurdle they overcome is another step toward greater strength. They train their minds to see adversity as an opportunity to grow, adapt, and push past perceived limits—expanding their ability to handle future obstacles.

Growth Mindset

Develop a positive, growth-oriented mindset that empowers you to handle anything life throws your way. Believe in your ability to overcome, survive, and succeed. When you commit yourself to a goal, your mindset will fuel your ability to endure, adapt, and conquer. Strengthen this mindset daily through visualization, determination, and relentless hard work.

Navy SEALs adopt a "sustained forward movement" mentality—embracing challenges rather than shying away from them. The phrase, "Good to go" is a Navy SEAL's mental checkpoint which signifies readiness to keep pushing, no matter the task's difficulty. In the face of adversity, this mindset drives them to confront obstacles head-on, making action the default response instead of retreat or indecision. Whether physical, tactical, or mental, Navy SEALs are trained to take on challenges, pushing themselves forward and overcoming whatever is in their path.

Staying Calm Under Pressure

Navy SEALs are experts at maintaining composure and making sound decisions under extreme pressure. Their ability to stay cool in high-stress environments is not just a natural trait—it is the result of rigorous training, strategic thinking, and a disciplined mindset. By developing mental resilience, practicing stress inoculation, and mastering the art of patience, Navy SEALs ensure they can operate effectively, even when the stakes are life or death.

Navy SEALs are trained to think on their feet and adapt to real-time challenges. In high-pressure situations, plans often change, and new obstacles arise. Rather than panicking, Navy SEALs assess the situation, adjust their approach, and execute the best course of action based on the evolving conditions. They rely on a combination of planning, improvisation, and teamwork to turn unexpected challenges into opportunities for success.

In both combat and life, rushed decisions often lead to costly mistakes. Navy SEALs cultivate patience because they understand that true success requires endurance, careful planning, and methodical execution. Whether gathering intelligence for months or waiting for the perfect moment to strike, they know that discipline and timing are just as critical as action itself.

Patience also plays a key role in team dynamics. Trust is not built overnight—it requires consistent, sustained actions over time. Navy SEALs recognize that strong team relationships, much like successful missions, require patience and dedication.

Peak Performance Requires Rest

Peak performance isn't just about pushing limits—it's about smart recovery. Navy SEALs structure their training cycles to avoid burnout, incorporating active recovery, sleep, nutrition, and mental rest to sustain long-term resilience.

- **Active recovery days** prevent overtraining while keeping Navy SEALs engaged.
- **Mindset training** ensures they remain adaptable, composed, and mission-ready, even under extreme stress.

While mental and physical toughness is encouraged, Navy SEALs are also trained to recognize signs of overtraining, fatigue, or injury. Knowing when to recover is just as vital as pushing through adversity, ensuring longevity and peak performance.

Sleep, hydration, and nutrition are all essential to both mental and physical resilience. Navy SEALs often face extreme fatigue and sleep deprivation during operations, but they are trained to prioritize rest whenever possible. Sleep is critical for cognitive function, decision-making, and overall health.

They learn to take advantage of any opportunity to rest, even if it's just a short power nap. These brief naps help counteract sleep deprivation during missions or high-intensity training, providing the body with a much-needed recovery boost.

Make Time for Downtime

Recovery goes beyond physical techniques—it also includes mental downtime. **Navy SEALs understand the importance of stepping back to recharge from the relentless demands of training and operations.**

In some cases, recovery doesn't mean complete rest. Instead, Navy SEALs engage in light activities like swimming, mobility exercises, or low-intensity cardio such as cycling. These activities keep muscles loose, prevent stiffness, and aid recovery while maintaining active movement.

Hydration

Hydration is a fundamental pillar of physical and mental performance. Navy SEALs maintain a steady intake of water throughout the day, not just when they feel thirsty, as dehydration can lead to fatigue, muscle cramps, and cognitive decline—factors that can compromise mission success.

To prevent electrolyte imbalances that can cause cramping or fatigue, they also supplement their hydration with electrolytes.

Electrolytes form a fundamental pillar of physical and mental performance. Navy SEALs maintain a steady intake of fluids rich in electrolytes throughout the day, not just when they feel thirsty, as electrolyte depletion can lead to fatigue, muscle cramps, and cognitive decline—factors that can compromise mission success.

Nutrition

Proper nutrition is key to sustaining energy, supporting muscle repair, and optimizing cognitive function during training and operations. Navy SEALs follow a nutrient-dense diet that includes a balanced mix of:

- **Protein.** Essential for muscle recovery and repair, Navy SEALs prioritize high-quality protein sources such as lean meats, fish, eggs, and plant-based proteins to ensure they get the necessary amino acids to rebuild muscle tissue.
- **Complex carbohydrates.** Whole grains, vegetables, and fruits provide sustained energy throughout the day, preventing crashes associated with refined sugars. Navy SEALs rely on these carbs for long-duration endurance.
- **Healthy fats.** Sources like avocado, nuts, and olive oil support brain function and provide a steady, long-lasting energy source.

Navy SEALs strategically plan their meals to enhance performance. Before training or missions, they consume protein and carbohydrate-rich meals to fuel their bodies. After exercise, they focus on a balanced intake of protein and carbs to aid muscle recovery and replenish energy stores.

While whole foods are prioritized, Navy SEALs may use supplements to meet elevated nutritional demands during extreme training or missions. These supplements include protein powders, electrolyte tablets, and omega-3 fatty acids help support muscle recovery, hydration, and joint health.

Environmental Adaptation

Navy SEALs adjust their nutrition to match environmental conditions. In cold environments, they consume calorie-dense foods to offset increased energy expenditure. In hot climates, they focus on hydration and electrolyte replenishment to counteract fluid loss from excessive sweating.

Cold exposure, such as ice baths or cold showers, and contrast therapy (alternating hot and cold treatments) are common recovery techniques for Navy SEALs. These methods reduce muscle inflammation, accelerate recovery, and improve circulation by flushing out metabolic waste and bringing fresh oxygenated blood to muscles.

Mastering Mental and Physical Endurance

When faced with extreme fatigue, cold, and pain, Navy SEALs are trained to separate their minds from their bodies—acknowledging discomfort without allowing it to dictate their actions. They understand that the mind has the power to override the body's temporary suffering, enabling them to push forward even when they feel like they've reached their breaking point.

During physically demanding tasks, Navy SEALs recognize that exhaustion does not signal their true limits. Instead, they understand they have barely tapped into their full capacity. This mindset allows them to access deeper mental reserves, extending their endurance far beyond what they initially thought possible.

Whether facing a grueling 12-mile run, a six-mile swim, or hours of relentless exertion, Navy SEALs keep their focus on completing the next step rather than fixating on how much remains. By breaking challenges into smaller, manageable pieces, they prevent mental fatigue, stay motivated, and maintain forward momentum.

Quitting is Not an Option

At the core of Navy SEAL training is the unwavering belief that quitting is never an option. From day one, Navy SEALs are taught to take control of their mindset when the pain sets in. By cultivating a relentless "no quit" mentality, they train themselves to push through adversity, tapping into hidden reserves of energy when it matters most.

Navy SEALs know that true resilience is forged through repeated exposure to difficult situations. Each grueling training session is an opportunity to strengthen their ability to endure discomfort, fatigue, and adversity. This continual exposure rewires their brains, making them more adaptable and capable of handling extreme physical and mental stress.

Navy SEAL training incorporates relentless endurance exercises such as running with heavy loads, swimming in freezing waters, and enduring prolonged physical exertion. With each challenge, their mental and physical resilience strengthens, preparing them for even more demanding missions in the future.

Training Discipline

Navy SEALs don't train just for fitness—they train for discipline. Workouts are designed to push them past perceived limits, conditioning their minds to stay relentless in the face of discomfort. The mental endurance built through grueling physical challenges carries over into decision-making, leadership, and combat effectiveness.

- **Training for endurance, not perfection:** Navy SEALs sustain high performance over long durations, focusing on consistency rather than flawless execution.
- **Team-based workouts:** Training in teams reinforces mutual support, trust, and shared discipline.
- **Stress conditioning:** Navy SEALs push themselves to exhaustion, then make critical decisions—training their ability to perform under extreme pressure.

Through relentless training, Navy SEALs develop not just exceptional physical strength, but the unbreakable mindset necessary to succeed in the most extreme conditions. **Their philosophy is clear: consistency, resilience, and functional fitness forge elite warriors.**

Embracing Adversity

For Navy SEALs, resistance is an essential component of personal development. Navy SEALs train to maintain focus and determination even in the face of overwhelming adversity. **Every hardship is a lesson in resilience, making them more equipped to handle future challenges.** By reframing difficulties as necessary trials for growth, they continue to push forward, stronger and more prepared for whatever comes next.

Resistance is a force that forges strength. Navy SEALs demonstrate that the ability to push beyond limits, adapt in the face of setbacks, and reframe struggles as opportunities is what separates the successful from those who quit. In both life and combat, resilience is the ultimate weapon, and those who master it will find that no obstacle is insurmountable.

AFTER ACTION REVIEW

Mission Summary

For Navy SEALs, growth is forged through discomfort, persistence, and disciplined exposure to adversity. Navy SEALs succeed because they embrace pain, exhaustion, and uncertainty as essential elements of development. They cultivate mental toughness, focus on actionable steps, and refuse to let temporary discomfort derail their mission or personal progress.

Key Lessons for Reflection

Push Past Limits: Growth happens when you challenge yourself beyond the familiar and comfortable.

Embrace Discomfort: Pain, fear, and fatigue are tools for building resilience, not obstacles to avoid.

Mental Toughness and Resilience: Focus on the present moment and act despite discomfort.

Turn Obstacles Into Opportunities: Reframe challenges as steppingstones for personal and team growth.

Discipline and Training: Consistent exposure to difficult conditions develops endurance and prepares you for real-world challenges.

Recovery and Peak Performance: Rest, nutrition, and hydration ensure sustained high-level performance.

No Quit Mentality: Resilience is built through repeated exposure to hardship and refusing to give in to temporary relief.

Adaptability Under Pressure: Stay calm, think clearly, and adjust strategies when unexpected challenges arise.

Confirmation of Learning

- ✓ You understand that growth can be uncomfortable, intentional, and deliberate.
- ✓ You can identify strategies to turn adversity into opportunity in everyday life.
- ✓ You recognize the importance of discipline, preparation, and mental resilience in achieving sustainable success.
- ✓ You appreciate the role of rest, nutrition, and recovery in supporting long-term performance.
- ✓ By internalizing these lessons, you cultivate a mindset that not only endures discomfort but thrives in it. Like a Navy SEAL, you learn to confront challenges head-on, maintain focus under pressure, and emerge stronger from every trial. Growth is not accidental—it is earned through courage, persistence, and disciplined action.

"It pays to be a winner."

—Navy SEAL Aphorism

Hard work, discipline, and effort separate the best from the rest.

4

SURROUND YOURSELF WITH EXCELLENCE

To unlock your full potential, surround yourself with people who challenge you to be your best. Seek "swim buddies" and mentors who demand excellence from you, and avoid those who let you coast.

"Perfection is not attainable,
but if we chase perfection
we can catch excellence."

—Vince Lombardi

MISSION OBJECTIVES

This chapter focuses on elevating yourself through the people, principles, and practices around you. Navy SEALs understand that individual performance is inseparable from the team and environment. By surrounding themselves with disciplined, high-performing teammates, mentors, and leaders, Navy SEALs ensure constant growth, accountability, and excellence.

These concepts are directly applicable to personal and professional life. Surround yourself with people who challenge you, contribute to teams rather than just yourself, embrace mentorship, and cultivate leadership through integrity and service. Excellence is not achieved in isolation—it is built through the people you choose to influence you and the environment you operate in.

Learning Objectives

- Choosing the right people to challenge and inspire you.
- Building trust, collaboration, and shared responsibility under pressure.
- Leading through service, humility, empathy, transparency, and moral courage.
- Reading your environment, adapting in real time, and conveying information clearly.
- Passing down knowledge, reinforcing standards, and developing the next generation.

"Iron Sharpens Iron"

The best way to elevate yourself is by surrounding yourself with disciplined, high-performing individuals: "Iron sharpens iron." Navy SEALs push each other to be better, knowing that their environment shapes their success.

- **Surround yourself with those you respect and admire.** These are leaders, operators, or mentors who challenge you to improve. Elevate yourself by being around high achievers.
- **Embrace discomfort and discipline.** Growth comes from pushing beyond your limits.
- **Set high, unwavering personal standards.** Your habits define your success.
- **Take full responsibility for your actions.** No blaming, just solutions.
- **Find opportunity in every challenge.** Turn obstacles into steppingstones.

Teamwork

Teamwork is the foundation of success in high-performance environments, requiring trust, communication, and seamless collaboration to achieve collective goals. In the Teams, teamwork is essential for survival. Navy SEALs operate in extreme, high-pressure situations where they rely on each other to overcome obstacles and endure physical and mental challenges.

Teamwork is built on mutual trust and shared responsibility. Navy SEALs know that their teammates depend on them to act decisively and effectively, making it easier to push through adversity. This camaraderie ensures that no one faces hardship alone—supporting one another becomes second nature. In the Navy SEAL community, action is always the default response, and resilience is reinforced through collective effort.

Teamwork applies to all aspects of life. In the workplace, collaboration and trust make teams more effective. In relationships, strong teamwork fosters deeper connections. In communities, helping others and being a reliable friend strengthens bonds. **Teamwork is about leveraging strengths, communicating clearly, and always being there for those who count on you.**

Leadership and Teamwork in the Navy SEAL Teams

Every Navy SEAL is expected to step up and lead when the situation demands it, regardless of rank. This shared leadership responsibility fosters a culture of accountability, where each individual takes ownership of their role. By distributing leadership across the team, Navy SEALs ensure that every member is invested in the mission and understands how their contributions impact the overall success.

During operations, team leaders delegate specific tasks, empowering others to make real-time decisions. This decentralized approach ensures leadership is not confined to a single person but is instead shared throughout the team. Everyone is responsible for mission success, fostering a culture of collaboration and mutual trust.

Navy SEALs lead by example, demonstrating integrity in every action. In the Navy SEAL ethos, leadership and integrity are inseparable—high standards apply to both behavior and decisions. **Trust is the foundation of success, whether within the team or in external relationships.** By embodying integrity, Navy SEALs cultivate trust that extends beyond operations, forming the backbone of strong leadership.

Serving the Team First

A Navy SEAL leader shares success with their team, never seeking personal glory but instead recognizing the contributions of others. This approach fosters respect, trust, and unity within the group.

Leadership is about service, prioritizing the needs of the team over individual ambition. A humble leader who credits their team and remains open to feedback builds trust, strengthens the mission, and enhances team cohesion.

Leadership isn't about personal recognition but about guiding and empowering others. Navy SEAL leaders focus on team development, leading by example, and continuously improving the collective strength of their unit.

Navy SEAL leaders embody the team's core values—integrity, excellence, and accountability. They inspire trust by showing confidence in their team and empowering members to take ownership of their roles. Trust is a two-way street—leaders trust their team, and in return, team members trust their leaders. Delegating responsibility and encouraging autonomy further strengthen this bond.

Integrity is demonstrated in both success and failure. When mistakes happen, Navy SEAL leaders take full ownership, learn from them, and guide the team to do the same. This humility and accountability earn respect and reinforce team trust.

Moral courage is another defining trait. Navy SEAL leaders make tough decisions based on ethics, even when difficult or unpopular. By consistently doing what's right—often at personal cost—they inspire their team to follow suit.

Leadership Through Empathy and Communication

Empathy is essential in Navy SEAL leadership. Leaders understand the personal challenges their teammates may be going through and offer support when needed. This compassionate approach strengthens trust and fosters a positive, resilient team dynamic.

A Navy SEAL leader consistently upholds the values of honor, courage, and commitment, remaining steadfast in their principles. This reliability and dedication provide a strong foundation of trust for their team.

By continuously striving for excellence and leading with integrity, Navy SEAL leaders set the standard for their team, ensuring success in every mission they undertake.

Leadership Through Transparency

When a Navy SEAL leader makes a tactical decision, they take full responsibility for its outcome. The Navy SEAL leadership culture demands decisiveness and accountability, instilling confidence and unity within the team.

Honesty and transparency are essential to Navy SEAL leadership. Withholding information or minimizing problems erodes trust. Navy SEAL leaders communicate openly, sharing both successes and setbacks. This ensures the team remains informed, prepared, and capable of adapting to any challenge.

The Navy SEAL ethos instills a deep sense of personal responsibility in every aspect of life. **This culture of accountability drives continuous improvement,**

reinforcing resilience and commitment within the team. Whether in training or combat, Navy SEALs embrace lifelong learning and growth.

Leadership Through Service and Humility

True leadership in the Navy SEAL Teams is about serving others and prioritizing the team's needs above personal interests. A humble leader recognizes and values their teammates' contributions, fostering respect and trust. They remain open to feedback and never allow personal ego to interfere with mission success.

When a Navy SEAL leader receives recognition, they share it with their team, reinforcing a culture of mutual respect. They set the standard by demonstrating excellence in every task, no matter how small. Through their commitment to high standards, they inspire dedication to the mission and the well-being of their teammates.

A team-first mentality is at the core of Navy SEAL operations. Individual concerns take a back seat to the collective good. When challenges arise, teammates step up to support one another, adapt plans, and ensure mission success. This shared mindset strengthens unity and trust, making the team more resilient.

The Importance of Following Before Leading

Navy SEALs understand that learning to follow is just as critical as learning to lead. Following builds humility, discipline, and strong communication skills. By observing different leadership styles, Navy SEALs gain valuable insights into decision-making, accountability, and the challenges of command—preparing them for future leadership roles.

Being a good follower requires a strong work ethic and an unwavering commitment to excellence. Navy SEALs learn from both great leaders and those who struggle, refining their understanding of clear communication, responsibility, and adaptability. These lessons serve as a foundation for effective leadership.

Leadership carries immense responsibility, and Navy SEALs develop this understanding through experience as followers. This process deepens their grasp of accountability and moral courage, especially in high-stakes situations. When they step into leadership roles, they do so with humility, respect for their team, and the confidence to make tough decisions.

By mastering the art of following before leading, Navy SEALs cultivate essential qualities—humility, empathy, trust, and accountability—that define great leadership. This foundation enables them to inspire their teams, navigate adversity, and lead with unwavering integrity. The ability to follow first is what transforms

Navy SEALs into exceptional leaders, capable of guiding their teams to victory in any challenge.

Respect For Authority

Respect for authority is a fundamental principle of Navy SEAL training. Learning to follow before leading instills discipline, accountability, and an appreciation for leadership structures. **Navy SEALs understand that mission success depends on every team member fulfilling their role—whether as a follower or a leader.** This culture of mutual respect and trust strengthens team cohesion and ensures operational effectiveness.

Through exposure to different leaders during training, Navy SEALs learn various leadership styles, recognizing what works and what doesn't. They develop valuable skills in communication, task delegation, and team motivation. This diverse leadership experience enables them to adapt their approach to best support their team and mission objectives.

Situational Awareness

"Read the room and adapt." Navy SEALs excel in high-pressure environments by mastering focus, stress control, and adaptability. They differentiate between what they can control and what they cannot, allowing them to operate with clarity and precision. This balance is achieved through mental discipline, situational

awareness, and emotional control—critical elements that enhance effectiveness in any situation.

Situational awareness is a fundamental skill developed through rigorous Navy SEAL training. Navy SEALs continuously scan their environment, assess team dynamics, and evaluate changing circumstances. This ability enables them to make quick, informed decisions, even in uncertain and rapidly evolving conditions.

Navy SEALs apply situational awareness not only in combat but also in leadership and daily life. They develop a heightened sensitivity to their surroundings and the people around them, enabling them to anticipate challenges and adapt in real time. Whether responding to shifting intelligence, unpredictable weather, or evolving team dynamics, they are prepared to pivot instantly.

Pattern recognition is a key component of this awareness. Navy SEALs learn to detect irregularities in behavior or environmental factors that may signal potential threats. By identifying and analyzing these patterns, they mitigate risks before problems escalate.

Situational awareness extends beyond combat—it is just as essential in leadership roles. Through keen observation, active listening, and adaptability, Navy SEALs remain attuned to their environment, their team's needs, and external challenges. Their ability to "read the room" and adjust accordingly is a skill sharpened through years of experience and training.

Navy SEALs carry this skill into every aspect of life. It allows them to navigate complex environments, make quick, strategic decisions, and remain adaptable in any situation. Whether on the battlefield or in the boardroom, their ability to assess, respond, and lead effectively is a defining trait of exceptional leadership.

Communication

Navy SEALs adapt their communication style to fit the circumstances—using direct, concise commands when speed is critical and a more measured, motivational tone when reassurance is needed.

Clear communication is fundamental to mission success, safety, and coordination. In high-stakes scenarios, where split-second decisions determine outcomes, the ability to convey information precisely can mean the difference between success and failure. Here's why effective communication is vital:

- **Prevents costly mistakes.** In high-pressure environments, confusion can lead to errors with serious consequences. Navy SEALs eliminate ambiguity, ensuring that every team member fully understands their role, the mission objectives, and the operational landscape. This clarity prevents missteps that could escalate under stress. Clear, calm communication keeps the team focused and mission-driven, even in the most intense moments. When emotions run high, a steady voice and clear directives reduce panic and keep operations on track.

- **Ensures seamless coordination.** Complex missions demand flawless synchronization. Whether securing a building, executing a rescue, or maneuvering through hostile territory, precise communication ensures every team member understands their responsibilities and acts in unison. For example, in a hostage rescue, coordinated communication between entry teams, snipers, and extraction units is essential for success.
- **Strengthens teamwork and cohesion.** Strong communication fosters collaboration and trust. When every Navy SEAL can communicate effectively, the unit functions as a cohesive force. Open communication allows insights, concerns, and critical information to flow freely, enhancing collective problem-solving and adaptability.

Clear communication minimizes confusion, maintains focus, strengthens coordination, and fosters trust—allowing Navy SEALs to operate with maximum efficiency and effectiveness. Mastering communication is a defining trait of those who perform under pressure.

Leadership and Mentorship

Navy SEALs recognize that their greatest impact often lies in those they inspire and train. They take pride in setting an example of leadership, discipline, and resilience.

- By mentoring younger operators, they reinforce the standards of excellence.
- They pass down skills and wisdom that only experience can teach.
- Their influence ensures that the next generation is stronger, faster, and better prepared.

A Navy SEAL's mission extends far beyond the battlefield. One of the most powerful aspects of their purpose is mentoring and guiding the next generation of Navy SEALs. By sharing hard-earned lessons, refining skills, and instilling a warrior mindset, they ensure that the legacy of excellence continues. **Their why is not solely about personal achievement—it's about strengthening the team, the community, and the world around them.**

AFTER ACTION REVIEW

Mission Summary

Your environment, your relationships, and your leadership define your ability to excel. Navy SEALs succeed by intentionally surrounding themselves with high standards, fostering trust, and taking ownership of their actions. Leadership is inseparable from service, and teamwork is the backbone of mission success.

Key Lessons for Reflection

Elevate Yourself Through Others: Surround yourself with disciplined, high-performing individuals who challenge you to grow.

Teamwork is Non-Negotiable: Trust, communication, and collaboration are essential for collective success.

Lead Through Service and Integrity: Humility, empathy, and accountability define effective leadership.

Follow Before Leading: Learn the value of observing, supporting, and understanding leadership before assuming command.

Situational Awareness Matters: Assess environments, anticipate challenges, and adapt quickly.

Communication is Critical: Clear, concise, and context-appropriate communication ensures coordination and effectiveness.

Mentorship Extends Impact: Passing knowledge, reinforcing standards, and guiding others ensures long-term success.

Confirmation of Learning

- ✓ You recognize that excellence is cultivated through people, relationships, and intentional habits.
- ✓ You understand the importance of trust, communication, and shared responsibility for both individual and team success.
- ✓ You appreciate that effective leadership combines service, integrity, and accountability.
- ✓ You can identify strategies to mentor, influence, and develop others while maintaining your own growth trajectory.
- ✓ By internalizing these lessons, you create an environment that elevates performance, fosters resilience, and reinforces high standards. Like a Navy SEAL, you learn that personal excellence is inseparable from the quality of your team, your mentors, and your choices—and that success is built through deliberate, disciplined, and shared effort.

"You don't have to like it—
you just have to do it."
—Navy SEAL Aphorism

Discipline means executing, no matter how you feel.

5

OWNERSHIP & RESPONSIBILITY

Take full responsibility for your personal growth and success. Just like Navy SEALs, don't wait for external motivation—be proactive, set long-term goals, and stay focused on your development.

"Success is the ability to go from one failure to another without any loss of enthusiasm."

—Winston Churchill

MISSION OBJECTIVES

This chapter emphasizes taking full ownership of your life, actions, and outcomes, a principle at the core of Navy SEAL training and operational success. Navy SEALs understand that accountability is non-negotiable: success comes from proactive decision-making, unwavering discipline, and prioritizing the team over self.

These concepts translate into practical strategies for personal and professional growth: take ownership of your responsibilities, develop discipline, stay focused on what you can control, build reliable support systems, and approach life with purpose and integrity.

Learning Objectives

- Making confident decisions, adapting to changing conditions, and accepting responsibility for every outcome.
- Owning mistakes, learning from them, and inspiring respect through integrity and reliability.
- Leveraging accountability partners and putting the team above personal ambition.
- Establishing habits, routines, and consistency to enable high performance under pressure.
- Compartmentalizing challenges, controlling controllables, and maintaining calm under stress.
- Aligning actions with a higher "why," and embracing personal mastery and moral courage.

Leading Yourself and Others

Navy SEALs live by the principle of accountability. If they fail, they own it, learn from it, and improve. **There are no excuses, no blaming circumstances—just a relentless focus on fixing what needs to be fixed.**

Navy SEALs act with confidence and are accountable for their actions, understanding that indecision can be more harmful than making the wrong choice. Hesitation can lead to missed opportunities or dangerous situations.

Navy SEALs recognize that plans rarely go as expected. They own their ability to adapt—whether the mission changes unexpectedly or obstacles arise, they take responsibility for how they respond and adjust quickly.

When unforeseen circumstances, like equipment failure or a new threat, emerge, a Navy SEAL immediately takes ownership of how to handle it and ensures the mission continues smoothly. For example, if a Navy SEAL's shot placement is off, they don't blame the wind or their weapon—they correct their technique and adapt. The same principle applies to any aspect of life: **If something isn't working, take responsibility, make adjustments, and move forward with purpose.**

Passing blame is never an option. Navy SEALs foster a culture of accountability, encouraging every team member, regardless of rank, to take ownership of their role in the mission's success or failure. Even if others make mistakes, Navy SEALs reflect on their own role in the situation. They don't deflect responsibility to subordinates or external factors.

If a mission fails because of a team member's mistake, the leader focuses on how they could've better prepared the team to avoid it, never shifting blame to the individual.

Inspire Respect

Navy SEALs don't just hold themselves to high standards—they inspire those around them to rise to the occasion. **Respect is a core value, and it's demonstrated through fairness, integrity, and unwavering commitment to the team.**

Respect requires action:

- **Listening** to teammates and valuing their input.
- **Acknowledging strengths** and supporting one another.
- **Keeping promises** and leading by example.
- **Mentoring** junior teammates.

Swim Buddies

Navy SEALs use the buddy system—relying on accountability partners or "swim buddies"—to stay disciplined, push past their limits, and maintain high standards. The concept is simple but powerful: you are responsible for

Shared Responsibility

In Navy SEAL culture, accountability is shared. When a mission doesn't go as planned, Navy SEALs debrief together, take responsibility, and learn from the experience. This mindset fosters continuous improvement, ensuring that the team grows stronger after each operation.

A unified team is greater than the sum of its parts. Navy SEALs move with precision, responding to threats as one and relying on each other's expertise to execute the mission. **When everyone is aligned and working toward the same objective, the mission's success is far more certain than if individuals acted alone.**

The challenges Navy SEALs face—both physically and mentally—are grueling. A team-first mentality ensures that no one faces these hardships alone. In difficult moments, the team rallies, providing the support and motivation needed to push through.

If personal preferences conflict with team objectives, the mission always comes first. Navy SEALs willingly take on extra duties, adjust to new roles, and make personal sacrifices to ensure collective success. This selflessness builds deep trust, strengthening relationships within the team.

The team-first mentality is what enables Navy SEALs to achieve extraordinary results in the most high-pressure, high-risk environments. By prioritizing collective success over individual recognition, they ensure that every member contributes to the mission. Their strength lies in unity—working together toward a shared goal, trusting one another, and adapting to overcome any challenge.

Discipline is Freedom

Discipline is not about occasional motivation—it's about establishing non-negotiable habits and is the foundation of success. Freedom comes from mastering self-control, building routines, and eliminating excuses. By developing strict habits, progressively increasing difficulty, and focusing on consistency, Navy SEALs create a structure that allows them to perform at their highest level—no matter the challenge.

Navy SEALs operate with an unbreakable dedication to continuous learning, rigorous training, and personal growth, knowing that every day they are not improving, the enemy is. True discipline extends beyond motivation—it is the ability to stay focused and execute objectives regardless of adversity, fatigue, or external pressures. **Navy SEALs master this through consistent routines, accountability, and integrity, ensuring that they follow through on their commitments and uphold the highest ethical standards.**

Navy SEALs inspire trust not through words, but through actions—setting the standard by demonstrating discipline in every aspect of their lives. Trust is built through reliability, consistency, and adherence to core values, even in life-or-death situations.

Discipline Requires Commitment

Discipline also means pushing beyond comfort zones, embracing challenges, and staying committed to self-improvement. Whether it's waking up at 4:30am for training, executing a mission with precision, or making split-second decisions under pressure, Navy SEALs do not deviate from their objectives. Their ability to control emotions, eliminate distractions, and remain mission-focused ensures their success, both in combat and in life.

Start small and scale up. Begin with basic habits and progressively increase difficulty:

- **Physical Training:** Start with foundational PT (push-ups, pull-ups, running) and **increase intensity over time**.
- **Mental Resilience Training:** Begin with five minutes of **breath control** and expand into **visualization and stress inoculation techniques**.
- **Task Discipline:** Set **daily goals**, complete them no matter what, and gradually increase complexity.

Discipline is the key to freedom—when you control your habits, mindset, and actions, **you remove chaos and uncertainty, allowing yourself to operate with precision and effectiveness in any situation.** Develop rigid daily habits that become part of your life—no excuses. Set a strict daily routine and stick to it, regardless of circumstances.

The ability to push past physical and mental limits is at the core of Navy SEAL training. Navy SEALs unlock their hidden potential by mastering the mental game—embracing discomfort, controlling their mindset, and relying on their mental toughness. This mindset enables them to go beyond what they initially believed possible, continually raising the bar in terms of performance. This ability to push through barriers is essential for their success, especially in extreme and high-stress environments.

Focus on the Fundamentals

This can be as simple as making a commitment to wake up early. Many elite performers—Navy SEALs, CEOs, and entrepreneurs—wake up early to gain an advantage over the day. Early mornings are free from distractions, allowing for deep focus on high-priority tasks.

Maintain consistency—no excuses. *"Plan your dive and dive your plan,"* or in other words, once a plan is set, follow through regardless of motivation. This also means holding yourself accountable. **Track progress, measure results, and keep yourself honest when it comes to meeting your own standards.**

Control the Controllables

Navy SEALs stay focused on what they can control, rather than stressing over what's beyond their reach. In any situation, they assess their immediate environment, tackle what's within their power, and disregard everything else.

By doing so, they avoid the mental clutter of hypotheticals and future outcomes. In a firefight, for example, Navy SEALs will focus solely on the next task—finding cover, adjusting their position, and making decisions based on the current situation—rather than stressing over the bigger picture or uncontrollable factors like the weather.

- **They focus on what they can control** and take full responsibility for outcomes.
- If a mission is delayed or equipment fails, Navy SEALs **adapt, stay prepared, and adjust their plan.**
- **Break tasks into manageable steps.** Instead of being overwhelmed, ask: *"What can I control right now?"*
- **Overcome obstacles with action.** If you encounter an unexpected challenge, **reassess, communicate, and find a new path forward.**
- **Let go of external distractions.** *"Control the controllables."* Focus on **what you can influence,**

such as training, preparation, and mindset, while ignoring factors beyond your control.

Compartmentalize

Navy SEALs use the technique of compartmentalization to break overwhelming challenges into smaller, more manageable steps. By focusing on one task at a time, prioritizing their actions, and maintaining a clear direction, Navy SEALs reduce anxiety and avoid feeling overwhelmed. In high-pressure situations, this approach keeps them focused, calm, and in control.

This process involves mental discipline—mentally separating each task and focusing on it fully, whether it's a physical challenge, a tactical move, or a decision under pressure. They don't let the scale of a situation cloud their judgment.

Navy SEALs prioritize actions based on the most immediate needs. When everything is happening at once, they rely on their ability to take action, step by step. **By mastering the mental game and continuously pushing beyond their limits, Navy SEALs unlock new reserves of strength and endurance, enabling them to perform at the highest level even in the most intense circumstances.** Each completed step builds momentum, reinforcing their focus and keeping them grounded in the present task.

Whether it's navigating through harsh environments or making critical decisions under pressure, this approach allows them to stay effective, calm, and in control—qualities that are crucial for success in the most challenging situations.

Living with Purpose: The Navy SEAL Mindset

For Navy SEALs, living with purpose is the foundation of their mental and physical endurance. Their resilience is fueled by a deep understanding of their "why"—a driving force that extends beyond the mission at hand to a greater sense of duty, honor, and service.

Navy SEALs are motivated by an unwavering commitment to protect their comrades, defend national interests, and stand up for those who cannot defend themselves. Their purpose is deeply rooted in service—to their team, their country, and a cause greater than themselves.

- **"Never leave a man behind"** is more than a saying; it's a core belief that guides every decision.
- **Personal sacrifice** is accepted as necessary for the success of the team.
- **The mission always comes first,** reinforcing their commitment to mission success.

Navy SEALs don't just train to be strong; they train to be the best versions of themselves—physically, mentally, and emotionally. Their why is rooted in personal mastery, pushing their limits to refine skills, strengthen resilience, and improve as individuals.

- **Every challenge** is seen as an opportunity for growth.
- **Training is not just preparation**—it's a path to self-improvement.
- **Excellence** is not a destination but a lifelong commitment.

Living with Honor and Integrity

Navy SEALs prioritize honesty, integrity, and moral uprightness in all areas of life. **Honor means doing what's right, even when no one is watching.** Navy SEALs ensure their actions reflect this value by maintaining high standards of behavior both on or off duty. Every decision is guided by an internal compass of integrity—whether giving their best effort in training or making ethical decisions in everyday life, Navy SEALs choose to act with honor in all circumstances.

AFTER ACTION REVIEW

Mission Summary

Ownership and responsibility are the engines of personal and team excellence. Navy SEALs succeed because they take initiative, act decisively, and remain accountable—no excuses, no blame-shifting. Discipline, focus, and a team-first mentality reinforce every action, creating a culture of trust, performance, and resilience.

Key Lessons for Reflection

Own Everything: Take responsibility for your growth, decisions, and outcomes. Avoid blaming others or circumstances.

Lead and Follow: Lead when needed, but respect authority and learn by observing others first.

Accountability: Learn from mistakes, adapt, and improve continuously.

Team-First Mentality: Prioritize collective success, support your teammates, and rely on accountability partners.

Discipline and Habits: Build structured routines, focus on fundamentals, and maintain consistency.

Control the Controllables: Focus on actions within your power, adapt to challenges, and maintain calm under pressure.

Mental Mastery: Compartmentalize tasks, push beyond discomfort, and maintain clarity in high-stress situations.

Purpose, Honor, and Integrity: Let your "why" guide your actions, uphold moral standards, and act with honor even when unseen.

Confirmation of Learning

- ✓ You recognize that ownership begins with mindset and daily habits.
- ✓ You understand that discipline, accountability, and teamwork amplify performance.
- ✓ You appreciate that purpose and integrity are non-negotiable for sustainable success.
- ✓ You can identify practical ways to apply these principles in everyday life, from work to relationships to personal development.
- ✓ By internalizing these lessons, you create a foundation for reliability, resilience, and excellence—ensuring that you, like a Navy SEAL, can navigate adversity, take decisive action, and inspire others to rise to the challenge.

"Get comfortable being uncomfortable."

—Navy SEAL Aphorism

Success requires pushing beyond limits and thriving in adversity.

6

IDENTIFYING YOUR MISSION

Clearly define what truly matters and prioritize actions that lead to success.

"If my mind can conceive it,
if my heart can believe it, then
I can achieve it."

—MUHAMMAD ALI

MISSION OBJECTIVES

This chapter focuses on clarity of purpose, strategic thinking, and decisive action, skills that are essential for Navy SEALs and invaluable for anyone striving to achieve meaningful goals. Navy SEALs operate in high-stakes environments where success depends on breaking down complex challenges, maintaining focus under pressure, and acting decisively even in the face of fear or uncertainty.

These principles translate into practical strategies for achieving goals, managing stress, navigating challenges, and improving decision-making in life, work, and relationships. By identifying priorities, breaking tasks into actionable steps, and practicing visualization, anyone can operate with focus, confidence, and purpose.

Learning Objectives

- Clearly identify what truly matters and prioritize actions that lead to success.
- Break overwhelming challenges into manageable steps to maintain focus and momentum.
- Develop the ability to assess situations quickly, make informed decisions, and act decisively.
- Adapt to unexpected challenges with flexibility, innovation, and resourcefulness.
- Use mental rehearsal to build resilience, confidence, and readiness for high-pressure scenarios.

- Stay attuned to teammates' needs, leveraging compassion and accountability to strengthen the collective effort.
- Take action over hesitation, control the controllables, and maintain clarity in complex or stressful situations.

Break Down Challenges

Challenges—especially physical challenges like long runs, carrying heavy gear, or enduring extreme conditions—can seem overwhelming, but Navy SEALs tackle them one evolution at a time. For instance, on a long ruck march, they focus on reaching the next checkpoint rather than the entire distance. **This focused approach allows them to maintain mental clarity and continue pushing forward.**

Task Segmentation

When tasked with complex missions—like clearing a building—Navy SEALs break the operation into smaller, more manageable steps:

- Enter the building safely
- Secure the first room
- Clear subsequent rooms one at a time
- Communicate with the team to adjust tactics as needed
- Neutralize threats

By focusing on these individual actions, Navy SEALs prevent themselves from becoming overwhelmed by the complexity of the mission.

Strategic Thinking and Courageous Action

Developing strategic thinking is essential for navigating complex situations, especially when facing uncertainty or high-pressure environments. Navy SEALs are trained to quickly assess a situation and choose the most effective course of action, always considering the long-term goals and potential consequences. This skill is cultivated through tactical exercises, where they are required to make fast decisions with limited information. These situations teach Navy SEALs to trust their instincts, rely on their extensive training, and avoid becoming paralyzed by overthinking. In moments of crisis, their ability to evaluate options quickly and effectively is crucial for success.

One of the key elements of Navy SEAL training is the development of the ability to act decisively even in the face of fear. They are taught to recognize the physiological and psychological signs of fear, which can often lead to a "freeze" response. In combat, hesitation can be deadly. Therefore, Navy SEALs practice techniques to break the freeze response, such as controlled breathing and mental focus, ensuring that they transition from fear to decisive action swiftly. **This is critical, as in**

real-world situations, hesitation can lead to missed opportunities or increased danger.

Creative Problem-Solving for Unexpected Challenges

In the face of unexpected challenges, Navy SEALs rely on creative problem-solving to find solutions. They are trained to think on their feet, adjusting strategies when things don't go as planned, and leveraging the resources at hand to navigate obstacles effectively. **Their ability to stay flexible and innovative under pressure helps them remain calm and focused on the bigger picture, rather than becoming overwhelmed by the situation.**

Choose Your Battles

Choosing your battles wisely is another principle that Navy SEALs live by. They focus their energy on what truly matters and avoid wasting time on minor distractions. By prioritizing their efforts, they ensure that their actions are aligned with the mission and that they're not bogged down by unnecessary conflict. **Self-control is key—Navy SEALs practice restraint, focusing their energy only on the battles that will make the greatest impact.**

This sense of duty and accountability extends to personal reflection. Navy SEALs understand that growth requires self-awareness and constant improvement. They regularly take time to reflect on their actions, behaviors, and beliefs, making necessary adjustments to stay aligned with their purpose and values. Reflection is an active process—it's about learning from past experiences, seeking feedback from trusted teammates, and using those lessons to fuel future growth.

Empathy Means Staying Aware

In the high-pressure environments that Navy SEALs navigate, empathy and compassion are essential. They understand that everyone is facing their own challenges and that being supportive, and compassionate helps build stronger bonds within the team. Whether it's noticing a teammate who is struggling with stress or responding to emotional cues in a high-stakes situation, Navy SEALs always stay attuned to the needs of those around them.

By surrounding themselves with high performers and people who hold them accountable, Navy SEALs ensure they continue to grow and improve. Accountability is more than just a tool for success; it's a mindset that drives Navy SEALs to operate at their highest potential. They don't fight alone, and they don't grow alone—they are always pushing each other to become better, stronger, and more resilient.

Embrace Action Over Inaction

One of the core principles of Navy SEAL training is that action is always preferable to inaction. Even when making a wrong decision, taking action is seen as more productive than hesitation. Navy SEALs are taught to break through fear or doubt by repeating positive affirmations like "I can handle this," "Stay calm and focused," and "Take action now."

Trust the Process

Navy SEALs are taught that waiting for the "perfect" decision can paralyze them, so they focus on taking action and adjusting as needed. **Whether in training or in combat, they make decisions based on available information and proceed, knowing they can adapt if circumstances change.**

Maintain a Sense of Purpose

A deep sense of purpose and mission focus is critical for Navy SEALs. By staying clear on their mission, they make decisions with confidence, understanding how their actions contribute to the larger goal. **When the mission is clear, decision-making becomes straightforward, and distractions fall away.**

Avoid Paralysis by Over Analysis

Navy SEALs are trained to trust their instincts and avoid overanalyzing situations. Navy SEALs understand that their ability to make quick decisions impacts their team's morale. In high-stress environments, the danger of hesitation can cause doubt among their team members, and any delay to action can be life-threatening, so they make quick decisions and adapt based on real-time feedback. By making confident, swift decisions, leaders set the tone and maintain clarity in action. This instinctive decision-making helps them stay decisive, even when the situation is chaotic.

Setbacks can cause some individuals to freeze or overanalyze the situation, leading to missed opportunities. **Navy SEALs are trained to avoid paralysis by over analysis. Instead of getting stuck in indecision or fear of failure, they focus on taking decisive action.** Flexibility means making adjustments quickly and continuing to move forward, which is crucial for avoiding bigger problems down the line.

In a mission that hits a snag, Navy SEALs don't waste time overthinking. They adjust their plan, communicate with their team, and keep moving forward, knowing that indecision can lead to greater risks.

Visualization as Mental Conditioning

Visualization is a vital technique used to enhance performance, sharpen skills, and prepare for challenges. It strengthens mental readiness, improves resilience, and optimizes performance by allowing individuals to mentally simulate experiences and outcomes.

Navy SEALs rely on visualization to prepare for the intense demands of their missions. This mental rehearsal involves vividly imagining each step of an operation, anticipating obstacles, and envisioning a successful outcome. By practicing in their minds, Navy SEALs boost confidence, reduce anxiety, and enhance focus.

By envisioning high-stress scenarios—such as combat, physical exhaustion, or chaotic environments—Navy SEALs train their minds to remain calm and perform under duress. This mental conditioning strengthens confidence, ensuring they can manage fear, frustration, and uncertainty without being derailed.

Navy SEALs also use visualization to prepare for unpredictable crises. They imagine situations where plans go wrong—equipment failure, communication breakdowns, or sudden mission changes. Through mental practice, they develop adaptability, quick problem-solving, and the ability to stay composed in adversity.

Rather than solely picturing success, Navy SEALs focus on visualizing the process of completing each task.

They mentally walk through the entire mission, step by step, making adjustments as needed. This approach keeps them grounded in the present, reducing anxiety about the outcome and reinforcing focus on what they can control.

Visualization allows Navy SEALs to "experience" situations before they happen, making them more prepared to respond effectively under stress. They mentally walk through each step, seeing every detail—what they will do, how they will do it, and how they will overcome challenges. This "mental inoculation" against stress builds resilience, preventing real-life pressure from becoming overwhelming.

Visualization for Increased Resilience

To fully immerse themselves in visualization, Navy SEALs incorporate sensory details—imagining the sounds of gunfire, the discomfort of exhaustion, or the weight of their gear. This sensory realism conditions their minds and bodies to handle stress and discomfort more effectively.

Visualization is a powerful tool for unlocking hidden reserves of energy and endurance. By picturing themselves overcoming obstacles, Navy SEALs reinforce mental toughness and prepare their bodies to push through extreme conditions. Before physically demanding tasks, they visualize success, strengthening their confidence and determination.

This technique is often combined with relaxation strategies like deep breathing. Navy SEALs visualize themselves taking slow, controlled breaths in high-stress moments, regulating their heart rate and preventing panic. This integration of mental imagery and breath control ensures composure under pressure.

Through consistent practice, Navy SEALs transform high-stress situations into manageable challenges. By mentally rehearsing success, adapting to adversity, and controlling stress responses, they ensure peak performance when it matters most.

AFTER ACTION REVIEW

Mission Summary

Clarity of mission and decisive action are critical to success. Navy SEALs excel because they define their objectives, break down complex tasks, maintain situational awareness, and act decisively, even under pressure. They combine mental discipline, visualization, and team awareness to overcome fear, adapt to adversity, and achieve objectives efficiently.

Key Lessons for Reflection

Define Your Mission: Know what truly matters and align your actions with meaningful objectives.

Segment Challenges: Break complex tasks into smaller, actionable steps to prevent overwhelm.

Act Decisively: Avoid hesitation and trust your training, preparation, and instincts.

Creative Problem-Solving: Adapt strategies, leverage resources, and remain flexible under pressure.

Visualization: Mentally rehearse challenges to build resilience, confidence, and readiness.

Prioritize Wisely: Focus on battles that matter, avoid distractions, and allocate energy effectively.

Team Awareness and Empathy: Observe, support, and communicate with others to strengthen collective success.

Control the Controllables: Focus on what you can influence, adjust to setbacks, and maintain clarity under stress.

Mental Discipline: Compartmentalize tasks, push past discomfort, and maintain focus on the present.

Purpose-Driven Action: Let a clear sense of mission guide decisions, providing motivation, direction, and confidence.

Confirmation of Learning

- ✓ You can identify what truly matters and prioritize accordingly.
- ✓ You understand how to break overwhelming challenges into actionable steps.
- ✓ You appreciate the importance of decisive action, adaptability, and mental conditioning.
- ✓ You can apply visualization, focus, and empathy to improve performance in daily life and professional environments.
- ✓ By internalizing these lessons, you develop the clarity, courage, and resilience to navigate complex challenges, make confident decisions, and achieve your mission—just like a Navy SEAL.

7

ELIMINATING DISTRACTIONS

Remove anything that does not contribute to achieving mission success.

"It is during our darkest moments that we must focus to see the light."

—Aristotle Onassis

MISSION OBJECTIVES

This chapter focuses on maintaining focus, building mental fortitude, and embracing adaptability—core skills that enable Navy SEALs to perform at their peak in high-pressure environments. Navy SEALs face unpredictable conditions, high-stakes missions, and extreme stress, so their ability to eliminate distractions, manage fear, and remain composed is essential for mission success.

These principles translate into practical strategies for improving focus, resilience, and adaptability. By identifying and eliminating distractions, taking calculated risks, and staying calm under pressure, anyone can enhance productivity, make better decisions, and thrive in both personal and professional life.

Learning Objectives

- Staying fully present in chaotic situations to make rational, effective decisions.
- Developing resilience through stress inoculation, training under realistic conditions, and reframing challenges as opportunities.
- Adjusting quickly to new situations and turning uncertainty into growth opportunities.
- Taking full accountability and focusing on solutions rather than blame.

- Evaluating risks, confronting fears, and taking calculated actions to strengthen confidence and resilience.
- Pushing beyond personal limits, staying humble, and maintaining a team-first mindset.
- Remaining calm, decisive, and strategic when facing complex or high-stress challenges.

Block Out Unavoidable Distractions

Navy SEALs train to block out distractions and remain fully present in high-stress situations. This heightened focus allows them to accurately assess their surroundings and make rational decisions, even in chaotic environments.

For example, in the heat of battle, a Navy SEAL leader does not allow fear, frustration, or external chaos to cloud their judgment. Instead, they remain level-headed, prioritize objectives, and lead their team with clarity and confidence.

Navy SEALs also embrace the philosophy that some battles are marathons, not sprints. Whether it's years of preparation for a mission or the grueling process of becoming an elite operator, they understand that mastery requires consistent effort, resilience, and a focus on the journey, not just the outcome.

Rather than rushing through tasks, Navy SEALs emphasize precision, learning, and growth. This commitment to the process ensures that they are always improving, adapting, and pushing themselves toward long-term excellence.

Mental Fortitude

Mental fortitude is the ability to stay calm, focused, and decisive under pressure. Navy SEALs develop this skill through methods like intense training, stress inoculation, and disciplined mindset conditioning. Their ability to maintain composure in high-stakes situations isn't just about physical toughness—it's about training the mind to withstand adversity, block out distractions, and operate effectively under stress.

Key techniques for building mental fortitude include:

- **Stress Inoculation Training (SIT):** Navy SEALs expose themselves to progressively more intense stressors, allowing their minds and bodies to adapt over time. By intentionally placing themselves in uncomfortable and high-stress environments, they train to stay composed in real-world operations.
- **Visualization and Mental Rehearsal:** Before missions, Navy SEALs mentally rehearse complex tasks, picturing themselves executing each step successfully. This preparation builds confidence and reduces anxiety when facing real stress.
- **Breaking Down Challenges:** Instead of being overwhelmed by the big picture, Navy SEALs

focus on small, manageable steps. This method keeps them calm and ensures steady progress, even in chaotic situations.

- **Training Under Realistic Conditions:** i.e., Live-fire exercises, hostage rescue training exercises, and underwater demolition drills simulate combat stress, forcing Navy SEALs to develop the ability to think clearly and act decisively under extreme pressure.
- **Reframing Stress:** Navy SEALs don't see stress as an obstacle—they see it as a test of their resilience. They train to view discomfort as temporary, knowing that pushing through adversity strengthens both mind and body.
- **Team Trust and Support:** Navy SEALs rely on their teammates to maintain composure under pressure. Knowing they are not alone reduces anxiety and sharpens focus on their individual roles.
- **Reframing Stress as Growth:** Navy SEALs don't see obstacles as roadblocks but as opportunities to test their resilience. By viewing setbacks as steppingstones toward mastery, they maintain a positive, focused mindset.
- **Pushing Beyond Physical and Mental Limits:** During grueling runs and other endurance training evolutions, Navy SEALs remind themselves that pain is temporary, and pushing through it leads to greater strength, stamina, and mental resilience.

By consistently exposing themselves to challenging situations and conditioning their minds to endure pressure, Navy SEALs develop an unshakable mental resilience. **Mental fortitude is the key to staying focused and achieving success.**

Exposure to Stress Builds Resilience

By continuously facing stressors in training—night operations, extreme cold water swims, or high-risk missions—Navy SEALs become desensitized to pressure. This conditioning ensures their responses remain controlled and deliberate in real-world operations.

Navy SEALs don't view obstacles as setbacks but as opportunities to test their character and fortitude. They embrace adversity as a tool for self-improvement, knowing that every challenge they overcome strengthens their resilience.

Strive for Excellence

Navy SEALs are relentless in their pursuit of excellence, and their approach to lifelong growth can be applied to any area of life. By taking responsibility, focusing on solutions, and continuously adapting, anyone can build the resilience and discipline needed to succeed.

Mediocrity is unacceptable. If someone slacks off, their team holds them accountable. This discipline translates to all areas of life, reinforcing the importance of consistency, focus, and commitment to personal and professional growth.

For Navy SEALs, growth doesn't stop after graduating from BUD/s and receiving their Trident—it's a lifelong commitment. Their philosophy of, "Earn your Trident every day," reflects their mindset of continuous improvement.

Navy SEALs also don't let difficulties derail their progress. Instead of viewing setbacks as barriers, they treat them as temporary challenges that can be overcome with the right mindset and strategy. This approach keeps them moving forward rather than getting stuck in frustration or self-doubt.

Embrace Change by Cultivating Adaptability

Life is unpredictable, and those who can adapt—are the ones who thrive in any environment. Change can often trigger fear, especially when the unknown lies ahead. **However, Navy SEALs are trained to embrace change rather than resist it, seeing it as an opportunity for growth rather than a threat.** This mindset reduces anxiety, increases adaptability, and allows them to act decisively, even in uncertain situations.

Navy SEALs understand that personal and professional development comes from stepping outside of their comfort zone. Whether they are adapting to a new environment, mastering cutting-edge technology, or learning unfamiliar tactics, they recognize that embracing change strengthens their overall capabilities. **Stagnation leads to failure, while adaptability ensures success.**

Navy SEALs are constantly refining their strategies, adopting new technologies, and improving their training methods. They know that resisting change leads to obsolescence, while innovation and adaptability keep them ahead of potential threats. By maintaining an open mindset, Navy SEALs ensure that they are always improving and evolving.

Eliminate Passivity

Navy SEALs don't just adapt to change—they drive it. **By challenging conventional methods and embracing new ideas, they stay at the cutting edge of their craft.** Their ability to think outside the box and adopt the best strategies and technologies ensures they remain highly effective in every mission.

Navy SEALs train to quickly shift from a fixed mindset to a growth mindset when faced with obstacles. This allows them to embrace challenges, stay flexible, and remain effective under pressure. Instead of seeing change as a disruption, they view it as an opportunity to improve, innovate, and excel.

Navy SEALs recognize that change often brings new opportunities for success. By remaining flexible and open-minded, they enhance their effectiveness, improve team performance, and increase their ability to solve problems creatively. They don't see unfamiliar challenges as threats but as chances to expand their skill set and improve their overall readiness.

Applying Navy SEAL Adaptability to Everyday Life

- **Stay open to change**—embrace challenges as opportunities for growth.
- **Commit to continuous learning**—never stop improving your skills and knowledge.
- **Be proactive, not reactive**—adjust quickly and take control of new situations.
- **Turn setbacks into lessons**—use failures as steppingstones for success.
- **Maintain situational awareness**—always be prepared for unexpected shifts.

Change is a test of mental and emotional resilience. Navy SEALs have two choices when faced with new challenges: resist and struggle or embrace and grow. Their ability to adapt strengthens their resilience, allowing them to handle adversity—whether in combat, training, or life. Instead of allowing setbacks to create frustration, they analyze the lessons learned, adjust their approach, and move forward stronger than before.

By embracing change with confidence and resilience, Navy SEALs prove that adaptability is the key to thriving in any environment.

Stay Calm Under Pressure

In high-pressure situations, Navy SEALs focus on staying calm and in control. Instead of thinking, "I'm overwhelmed," they tell themselves, "I am focused. I will take this one step at a time." This internal shift helps them manage stress and pressure, maintaining their effectiveness even under the most intense conditions.

Navy SEALs are trained to accept that things won't always go as planned. Rather than seeking perfection, they focus on executing with the resources available and making necessary adjustments along the way. This mindset reduces stress and prevents them from getting caught up in irrelevant details. They understand that the goal is not flawless execution but rather effective, efficient action in the face of uncertainty. When a high-stress situation arises, such as a failure in communication equipment, Navy SEALs quickly adapt and focus on finding alternative solutions, letting go of the pursuit of perfection.

Remaining calm under pressure is crucial for effective situational awareness. Navy SEALs train to regulate their physiological responses, keeping their heart rate steady, controlling their breathing, and managing emotions—even in life-threatening situations. **This self-discipline ensures they can think clearly, make sound decisions, and maintain control in any environment.**

Eliminate Risk (Where Possible)

Develop the ability to realistically assess risks, distinguishing between legitimate concerns and irrational fears. When necessary, take calculated risks, evaluating potential rewards and consequences. Learn how to make informed decisions that help you navigate obstacles while minimizing negative outcomes.

Growth, success, and mission accomplishment often require stepping into the unknown and challenging the status quo. For Navy SEALs, risk-taking isn't about being reckless—it's about making thoughtful decisions to pursue larger objectives while remaining focused on the mission. Navy SEALs embrace this approach because they are trained to carefully evaluate risks, considering potential outcomes and consequences. They understand that taking calculated risks can sharpen their skills, helping them grow stronger. It's not about avoiding risk but about managing it wisely to overcome challenges in combat, training, and life.

By pushing boundaries and confronting their fears, Navy SEALs develop mental and physical resilience. These calculated risks lead to continuous improvement, preparing them for greater challenges throughout their careers. Without risk, there is stagnation.

Eliminate Comfort Zones

Growth and mastery require stepping outside of comfort zones. Navy SEALs know that avoiding risks keeps them stagnant, unable to advance toward their goals. Every risk—big or small—presents an opportunity to expand their abilities.

A Navy SEAL's long-term goals often involve mastering high-stakes operations, assuming leadership roles, or advancing in their careers. **The risks they take today, even if they result in failure or setbacks, lay the foundation for greater success in the future.** It's about long-term rewards, not short-term comfort.

For example, a Navy SEAL might push themselves beyond their physical limits during training, risking fatigue or injury, knowing that developing greater stamina will enable them to perform under pressure in future high-stress situations.

Risk-Taking as Team Building

Taking risks builds self-confidence and fosters trust within the team. When a Navy SEAL takes on a high-risk situation and succeeds, it boosts their belief in their abilities and instills confidence in the team. This trust is essential for success, especially in high-stakes operations. For instance, a Navy SEAL might take the risk of leading a mission in uncertain conditions, gaining valuable leadership experience that will serve them in future roles.

Trust is a cornerstone of Navy SEAL teamwork. Taking risks together—especially in high-stakes situations—strengthens bonds of trust and respect within the team. When a Navy SEAL takes a calculated risk and succeeds or fails with their team, it reinforces the value of shared responsibility and collective effort.

Navy SEALs understand that their long-term success is rooted in the strength and cohesion of the team. Taking risks together builds camaraderie and mutual reliance, which is critical when operating in life-threatening environments.

Manage Fear

Navy SEALs are trained to confront and manage fear, knowing that fear is often the biggest obstacle to success. By taking risks, they expose themselves to their fears, developing the courage to act under pressure.

Overcoming fear through risk-taking is an ongoing process that builds mental resilience, preparing Navy SEALs to remain calm under stress and make sound decisions when stakes are high. This is crucial for long-term survival and effectiveness in the field.

Navy SEALs understand that short-term discomfort and risk often lead to long-term rewards. They embrace risk because they know growth, success, and mastery require deliberate effort and sacrifice in the present. These risks develop essential skills, build confidence, foster innovation, and strengthen team cohesion. Navy SEALs don't shy away from risk; they embrace it as a critical tool for growth, improvement, and mission success. By aligning their actions with their long-term vision, they prepare themselves for greater challenges and higher levels of responsibility.

Remain Composed

In high-intensity situations, a Navy SEAL remains composed, assessing the situation objectively, weighing risks, and making clear-headed decisions. Their calm demeanor helps keep the team focused and adaptable.

Before a mission, Navy SEALs meticulously analyze potential obstacles and risks, creating contingency plans to address possible challenges. This risk management strategy ensures that the team can still achieve mission objectives despite unforeseen issues.

For Navy SEALs, courage isn't just physical bravery; it's also mental and moral courage to act in the face of adversity, doubt, or opposition. It's about confronting fear, taking risks, and doing what's necessary, even when it's daunting.

Eliminate Arrogance

Navy SEALs remain humble in success and driven by progress, embracing a mindset of continuous improvement and team-first thinking. In the Teams, ego is kept in check because no single operator is greater than the mission or the Brotherhood. Success is always attributed to the team, not the individual. **Navy SEALs know that complacency is the enemy, so they never rest on past accomplishments.** They are always seeking to refine their skills, push their limits, and learn from every experience.

Navy SEALs view adversity as part of the journey rather than something to fear. If something is outside their control, they reframe it as an opportunity to grow, adapt, or learn. This mindset shift allows them to release frustration and embrace challenges.

AFTER ACTION REVIEW

Mission Summary

Focus, mental resilience, and adaptability are critical to success. Navy SEALs excel because they actively eliminate distractions, confront fear, embrace challenges, and stay composed under pressure. Their disciplined approach transforms obstacles into opportunities, strengthens team cohesion, and ensures effective action even in chaotic or unpredictable environments.

Key Lessons for Reflection

Eliminate Distractions: Identify what truly matters and block out unnecessary noise or interruptions.

Build Mental Fortitude: Train the mind through exposure to stress, visualization, and breaking challenges into manageable steps.

Embrace Change and Adaptability: View uncertainty as an opportunity for growth and respond proactively.

Take Accountability: Eliminate excuses and focus on solutions rather than blame.

Manage Risk and Fear: Evaluate threats realistically, confront fears, and take calculated action.

Push Beyond Comfort Zones: Growth comes from stepping outside familiar boundaries and embracing challenge.

Stay Composed Under Pressure: Maintain calm, clarity, and focus to make sound decisions in stressful situations.

Eliminate Arrogance: Stay humble, maintain a team-first mindset, and continually pursue self-improvement.

Confirmation of Learning

- ✓ You understand how to identify distractions and maintain focus on your priorities.
- ✓ You can build resilience by facing challenges and adapting to change.
- ✓ You can take calculated risks, manage fear, and act decisively under pressure.
- ✓ You can embrace discomfort and growth while remaining humble and accountable.
- ✓ By internalizing these lessons, you develop the clarity, focus, and mental toughness to navigate complex challenges, maintain composure, and achieve your mission—mirroring the mindset of a Navy SEAL.

8

OPERATE WITH A MISSION SUCCESS MINDSET

Approach every challenge with focus, discipline, and determination.

"There is nothing impossible to they who will try."

—Alexander the Great

MISSION OBJECTIVES

This chapter centers on cultivating a mission-focused mindset, emotional control, and adaptive resilience—qualities that allow Navy SEALs to excel under extreme stress and uncertainty. Navy SEALs operate in high-stakes environments where pressure, unpredictability, and physical or mental fatigue are constants. Their ability to remain calm, disciplined, and purpose-driven ensures mission success and safety.

These Navy SEAL principles translate into practical tools for high performance under pressure: staying calm in stressful situations, adapting to change, focusing on priorities, and using setbacks as opportunities to grow.

Learning Objectives

- Maintaining focus on the immediate task to process information accurately and respond effectively.
- Adjusting strategies in real time when circumstances change, and maintaining flexibility in thought and action.
- Managing fear, frustration, and stress to stay composed and effective.
- Prioritizing key objectives, breaking complex tasks into manageable steps, and avoiding distractions.

- Using inner dialogue to maintain motivation, resilience, and determination.
- Understanding that success often comes through sustained effort and perseverance.
- Preparing for multiple scenarios and ensuring seamless execution of backup plans.
- Using training to simulate obstacles and develop strategies for overcoming real-world challenges.

Mindfulness in Navy SEAL Operations

Navy SEALs practice mindfulness to maintain focus, stay present in the moment, and eliminate distractions. This heightened awareness sharpens their ability to react swiftly to changing situations and make precise decisions under pressure, without becoming overwhelmed by external stressors.

In combat, Navy SEALs must be attuned to the smallest details—subtle shifts in their environment, changes in body language, or the slightest movements of an adversary. **Mindful awareness allows them to process this information rapidly and respond in real time, ensuring they are always prepared for the unexpected.**

Navy SEALs frequently operate in extreme environments, facing high stress and sleep deprivation. Mindfulness techniques play a crucial role in building resilience. Whether it's focusing on their breath during a grueling swim or maintaining mental presence during physically demanding tasks, mindfulness helps them remain grounded and avoid becoming overwhelmed by external pressures.

Beyond operational performance, mindfulness also enhances emotional control. Regular practice enables Navy SEALs to manage strong emotions such as fear, frustration, or anger—critical in high-stakes situations where composure can mean the difference between mission success and failure.

Adaptability Over Control

Plans rarely survive first contact with the enemy or adversity, and Navy SEALs are trained to accept that. When things go awry, the key is to adapt swiftly. Through rigorous contingency planning, they practice adjusting on the fly to unexpected changes. For instance, if weather conditions change or an enemy unexpectedly appears, Navy SEALs instantly switch to their backup plans, acting quickly and decisively. Waiting for perfect conditions is a road to failure; instead, Navy SEALs focus on adapting and pushing forward regardless of the circumstances.

Navy SEALs are trained to adapt—modifying their strategy and utilizing mental flexibility to find alternative solutions. This adaptability allows them to keep moving forward, regardless of the circumstances.

Managing emotions in high-stress situations is a critical skill for Navy SEALs. Emotional reactions, such as panic or frustration, can cloud judgment and reduce effectiveness. Navy SEALs practice techniques to control their emotions, ensuring they remain focused, calm, and clear-headed, even in chaotic environments.

When things fall apart—whether it's an injury, a broken plan, or a change in conditions—Navy SEALs remind themselves to stay calm. They focus on what they can do next, accepting that while they can't control the outcome, they can always control how they respond. Through deep breaths and focused actions, they stay composed and move forward with purpose.

Applying Navy SEAL-Level Composure to Everyday Life

By mastering emotional control, patience, and adaptability, Navy SEALs ensure that pressure becomes an advantage, not a weakness. Their ability to remain calm under extreme stress is what makes them some of the most effective warriors in the world—an approach that can be applied to any high-stakes situation in life.

- **Stay adaptable.** When faced with an unexpected challenge, adjust your approach instead of resisting change.

- **Practice patience.** Recognize that long-term success requires steady progress and perseverance.
- **Regulate emotions.** Train yourself to stay calm and focused, even in stressful situations.
- **Embrace strategic thinking.** Avoid knee-jerk reactions by assessing situations carefully before acting.
- **Develop resilience.** View setbacks as opportunities to learn and grow rather than as failures.

Focus on the Mission

Navy SEALs focus on mission success, keeping their eyes fixed on the commitment to succeed, regardless of the obstacles or discomfort that might arise along the way. **Their focus on mission success far outweighs any temporary feelings of doubt or fatigue.**

Resilience and Adaptability

Navy SEALs are trained to be resilient—embracing adversity, adapting to challenges, and moving forward. Their resilience is born from their deep commitment to their objectives, which allows them to keep pushing through tough situations without waiting for motivation to push them into action.

Long-Term Perspective

Success doesn't happen overnight. It takes years of consistent, demanding work to achieve their objectives. **Their commitment to long-term goals ensures they remain focused, even during moments of fatigue or doubt.** This long-term perspective helps them stay grounded and continue their mission, no matter how difficult the journey may get.

Focus on the Present

Rather than dwelling on past mistakes or worrying about the future, Navy SEALs focus on the task at hand. By staying present, they reduce anxiety and increase their ability to execute. For example, during a mission, they won't worry about the entire timeline but will focus on executing the next critical step.

Navy SEALs are trained to stay focused on what's immediately in front of them, avoiding the overwhelming weight of the bigger picture. When faced with a daunting challenge, they break it down into manageable tasks. For instance, during a mission, rather than dwelling on the entire operation, they focus solely on the next step—whether that's clearing a room, moving to a new position, or providing support for a teammate. This keeps them from getting mentally bogged down by the entire scope of the situation.

They prioritize tasks based on urgency and importance. They identify key objectives and break them down into smaller tasks that need to be completed in sequence. **This approach allows them to progress methodically, even when the overall situation feels chaotic.**

To stay organized under pressure, Navy SEALs use mental checklists. These break each phase of a task into smaller actions, which they can tick off one by one. This process helps them regain a sense of control and accomplishment, while preventing crucial details from slipping through the cracks.

Use Positive Self-Talk to Reframe Negative Thoughts

Navy SEALs are experts in using positive self-talk and mental reframing to stay motivated, even when faced with overwhelming challenges. When doubt, fatigue, or frustration creeps in, they consciously redirect their thoughts from negative to empowering. Instead of focusing on how tired or defeated they feel, Navy SEALs focus on their strength, resilience, and capability.

For example, when experiencing physical exhaustion, rather than thinking, "I can't go any further," they tell themselves, "I've trained for this, my mind is strong, my body is strong, and I can do this." This shift in mindset helps Navy SEALs push through moments of weakness, maintaining focus on their inner strength and determination.

Through consistent practice of positive self-talk, they reinforce their belief in their ability to overcome obstacles, no matter how difficult the situation may seem. **This mental reframing keeps them motivated, engaged, and moving forward.**

By making self-talk a tool for empowerment, Navy SEALs ensure that their minds remain as strong, or even stronger than their bodies, helping them break through mental barriers and perform at their peak when it matters most.

Cultivate Patience: "Some Battles Are Marathons, Not Sprints"

Navy SEALs understand that not every challenge is resolved quickly. Some missions or battles require sustained effort and long-term persistence. **Patience is a key part of their training, as they recognize that success often comes after repeated effort and overcoming obstacles over time.** They approach each task with the mindset of a marathon runner, knowing that steady, focused progress will lead to success.

Contingency Planning

In the Teams, there's a saying: "Be like Gumby—be flexible!" This mindset encourages adaptability in the face of shifting circumstances, ensuring that strategies are adjusted as needed to stay on course, whether in negotiations, confrontations, or other challenges. Navy SEALs understand that circumstances change, and the ability to adapt is essential to success.

Navy SEALs are trained to quickly adjust to new situations and when faced with the unexpected, they focus on what they can control rather than dwelling on things beyond their influence. **Rigidity can lead to failure, but adaptability often ensures survival and success.**

If a planned extraction route is blocked, Navy SEALs won't waste time on frustration. They quickly shift to an alternate route, check their equipment, or reassess the mission's objectives. The focus remains on executing the mission, no matter the changes.

By planning for multiple scenarios, they prepare for the unexpected and accept it as part of the mission. This allows them to let go of frustration over circumstances beyond their control and focus on the next best action. When a mission takes an unexpected turn, such as an enemy ambush, Navy SEALs rely on their contingency plans and shift to pre-prepared responses, without wasting time on what can't be changed.

"Practice" Failure

Navy SEALs practice failure scenarios during training—whether it's equipment malfunctions, communication breakdowns, or hostile engagements. Through these simulations, they develop backup plans for each scenario, ensuring that the mission can still proceed even if something goes wrong.

If a critical piece of equipment fails during a covert operation, the team quickly moves to Plan B. However, they don't give up on Plan A entirely. They continuously assess whether Plan A can still be salvaged and make necessary adjustments while executing the backup plan.

The success of Navy SEALs lies in their ability to create a Plan B that doesn't drastically deviate from Plan A. These alternatives ensure continuity, alignment with the broader mission goals, and the best chance of success, even if circumstances change. For example, in a mission to retrieve a high-value target, Plan A might involve a direct assault, while Plan B might focus on a stealth approach or an alternate entry point. Both plans aim for the same result—capturing the target—but adapt to the changing environment.

Plan as a Team

Rehearsing multiple contingencies ensures that the team can seamlessly transition between different strategies, without hesitation or confusion. **This preparedness helps them adapt quickly and effectively under pressure, ensuring the mission continues despite unexpected obstacles.**

Before a mission, the Navy SEALs on the team ensure that everyone is aligned on the main objectives and the contingency plans. If the need to switch to Plan B arises, there's no confusion or loss of momentum because everyone understands their role in the new strategy. This clear understanding ensures the team can execute the mission smoothly, no matter what challenges arise.

AFTER ACTION REVIEW

Mission Summary

Success under pressure isn't a skillset—it's a mindset. Navy SEALs excel not because they control every variable, but because they control how they respond. By cultivating mindfulness, emotional regulation, adaptability, and mission focus, they remain effective in chaotic environments. The ability to plan for contingencies, embrace failure, and maintain long-term perspective ensures continuous progress and resilience, both individually and as a team.

Key Lessons for Reflection

Stay Mindful: Focus on the present moment and eliminate distractions to enhance decision-making.

Adapt Quickly: Embrace change, adjust strategies as needed, and remain flexible in approach.

Control Emotions: Manage stress, fear, and frustration to maintain clarity and composure.

Prioritize the Mission: Keep your focus on key objectives and break complex challenges into actionable steps.

Use Positive Self-Talk: Reframe negative thoughts to reinforce resilience, confidence, and determination.

Practice Patience: Recognize that meaningful progress often requires sustained effort over time.

Plan for Contingencies: Prepare alternative strategies to remain effective when obstacles arise.

Train for Failure: Simulate setbacks in training or preparation to build adaptability and confidence.

Leverage Team Coordination: Ensure clear communication and alignment so the team can adjust without losing momentum.

Confirmation of Learning

- ✓ You can remain calm, focused, and present even under high pressure.
- ✓ You can adapt strategies proactively rather than resisting change.
- ✓ You can use mental techniques to maintain motivation and overcome setbacks.
- ✓ You can plan, execute, and adjust actions in alignment with your long-term objectives.
- ✓ By internalizing these lessons, you develop a mission success mindset: resilient, adaptable, focused, and decisive—a mindset that drives achievement not only in high-stakes operations but in every area of life.

"Make adversity your ally."

—Navy SEAL Aphorism

Challenges aren't roadblocks;
they're opportunities to become stronger.

CONCLUSION

IN TIMES OF WAR OR UNCERTAINTY, THERE IS A special breed of warrior ready to answer our nation's call. A common man with uncommon desire to succeed.

Forged by adversity, he stands alongside America's finest special operations forces to serve his country, the American people, and protect their way of life:

The United States Navy SEAL.

This book is intended as a blueprint for applying Navy SEAL principles to your everyday life, helping individuals develop the discipline, resilience, and mental toughness needed to excel in any endeavor. By embracing the Navy SEAL mindset and strategies, you will learn to stay focused under pressure, push past limitations, and pursue their goals with unwavering commitment.

Translating this elite warrior ethos, The Navy SEAL Code and Navy SEAL values, into practical, real-world strategies provides valuable lessons for people from all walks of life. Whether overcoming career challenges, personal setbacks, or refining self-discipline, you will gain the tools to perform at your peak—no matter the obstacles you encounter.

The Navy SEAL core values—discipline, teamwork, and resilience—serve as the foundation of their effectiveness in both combat and daily life. These values are not abstract ideals but guiding principles that shape every action, decision, and mission.

- **Discipline** ensures Navy SEALs maintain peak physical and mental readiness, executing operations with precision despite extreme conditions.
- **Teamwork** is the backbone of Navy SEAL operations, emphasizing trust, coordination, and mutual reliance to accomplish objectives and survive in hostile environments.
- **Resilience** defines a Navy SEAL's ability to push through pain, adversity, and overwhelming odds, never quitting until the mission is complete.

Beyond these core values, Navy SEALs integrate honor, courage, commitment, respect, excellence, selfless service, and adaptability into their daily actions. These values guide their decisions, shape their interactions, and reinforce their unwavering dedication to mission success. By embodying these principles, Navy SEALs maintain integrity, foster strong relationships, and uphold the highest standards of performance in all aspects of their lives.

THE NAVY SEAL CODE

Navy SEALs live by a code of discipline, honor, and performance:

- **Loyalty to country, team and teammate.**
- **Serve with honor and integrity, on and off the battlefield.**
- **Ready to lead, ready to follow, never quit.**
- **Take responsibility for your actions and the actions of your teammates.**
- **Excel as warriors through discipline and innovation.**
- **Train for war, fight to win, defeat our nation's enemies.**
- **Earn your Trident every day.**

THE NAVY SEAL TRIDENT

There is no finer or more apt symbol for the full spectrum of excellence embodied by the U.S. Navy SEAL than their insignia, the Trident. Each element of the Trident represents an aspect of their service. The eagle symbolizes the air. In its right talon is the trident itself—symbolic of Neptune, the Roman God of the sea. In the left talon is a cocked flintlock pistol, which symbolizes land warfare as well as a state of constant readiness.

For the U.S. Navy SEAL, the Trident is more than an emblem—it is an identity.

"Earn your Trident every day."

—Navy SEAL Aphorism

Yesterday's success doesn't matter—prove yourself daily.

THE NAVY SEAL ETHOS

"IN TIMES OF WAR OR UNCERTAINTY THERE IS a special breed of warrior ready to answer our Nation's call. Common citizens with uncommon desire to succeed. Forged by adversity, they stand alongside America's finest special operations forces to serve their country, the American people, and protect their way of life.

I am that warrior.

My Trident is a symbol of honor and heritage. Bestowed upon me by the heroes that have gone before, it embodies the trust of those I have sworn to protect. By wearing the Trident I accept the responsibility of my chosen profession and way of life. It is a privilege that I must earn every day.

My loyalty to Country and Team is beyond reproach. I humbly serve as a guardian to my fellow Americans always ready to defend those who are unable to defend themselves. I do not advertise the nature of my work, nor seek recognition for my actions. I voluntarily accept the inherent hazards of my profession, placing the welfare and security of others before my own.

I serve with honor on and off the battlefield. The ability to control my emotions and my actions, regardless of circumstance, sets me apart from others. Uncompromising integrity is my standard. My character and honor are steadfast.

My word is my bond.

We expect to lead and be led. In the absence of orders I will take charge, lead my teammates and accomplish the mission. I lead by example in all situations.

I will never quit. I persevere and thrive on adversity. My Nation expects me to be physically harder and mentally stronger than my enemies. If knocked down, I will get back up, every time. I will draw on every remaining ounce of strength to protect my teammates and to accomplish our mission.

I am never out of the fight.

We demand discipline. We expect innovation. The lives of my teammates and the success of our mission depend on me - my technical skill, tactical proficiency, and attention to detail.

My training is never complete.

We train for war and fight to win. I stand ready to bring the full spectrum of combat power to bear in order to achieve my mission and the goals established by my country. The execution of my duties will be swift and violent when required yet guided by the very principles that I serve to defend.

Brave SEALs have fought and died building the proud tradition and feared reputation that I am bound to uphold. In the worst of conditions, the legacy of my teammates steadies my resolve and silently guides my every deed.

I will not fail."

"Under pressure, you don't rise to the occasion—you sink to the level of your training."

—Navy SEAL Aphorism

Preparation and repetition make excellence automatic.

"If you are going through Hell,
don't slow down, stay focused
on the mission."

—Don Mann

ABOUT THE AUTHOR

Don Mann is a retired United States Navy SEAL veteran who served on SEAL Team ONE, TWO and SIX. After retiring from the Navy, he worked with numerous United States government agencies for over 25 years. He is the executive producer of the movie *The American Smuggler* and TV host of *Surviving Mann, The Mission* and *Face Off*. He has also authored over 20 books including the *New York Times* best-selling autobiography *Inside SEAL Team SIX*.

Don has over 40 years' worth of competitive extreme endurance racing experience, once completed two Ironman triathlons in a day and was ranked 38th in the world as a triathlete. He has climbed mountains all over the world and was injured while climbing Mount Everest.

Like this book?
Take a look.

navysealplaybook.com